Plant Magic

Plant Magic

A Celebration of Plant-Based Cooking for Everyone

Desiree Nielsen

PENGUIN

an imprint of Penguin Canada, a division of Penguin Random House Canada Limited

Canada • USA • UK • Ireland • Australia • New Zealand • India • South Africa • China

First published 2024

Interior illustrations: (blackberry) © yanushkov, (pepper and tomato) © nataleana, (mushroom) © Ansty Art, (avocado) © Armin Staudt, (cauliflower) © Vector Tradition, (pomegrante) © DashaKurinna, (lemon) © Наталья Выгузова, all stock.adobe.com; (kale) © JKB Stock, (artichoke) © nataleana, both Shutterstock.com

www.penguinrandomhouse.ca

LIBRARY AND ARCHIVES CANADA CATALOGUING IN PUBLICATION

Title: Plant magic : a celebration of plant-based cooking for everyone / Desiree Nielsen.
Names: Nielsen, Desiree, author.
Description: Includes index.
Identifiers: Canadiana (print) 20230200265 | Canadiana (ebook) 20230200281 |
    ISBN 9780735244900 (softcover) | ISBN 9780735244917 (EPUB)
Subjects: LCSH: Vegan cooking. | LCSH: Vegetarian cooking. | LCSH: Cooking
    (Natural foods) | LCGFT: Cookbooks.
Classification: LCC TX837 .N54 2024 | DDC 641.5/636—dc23

Cover and interior design by Andrew Roberts
Cover and interior photography by Gabriel Cabrera
Food and prop styling by Sophia MacKenzie

Printed in China

10 9 8 7 6 5 4 3 2 1

Contents

Introduction

It is not an understatement to say that my life has been transformed by deepening my relationship to plants, even when that was not the original intention.

   I went vegetarian as a teenager in hopes of impressing a boy—spoiler alert, it didn't work—but changing how I ate triggered a curiosity around what it means to be healthy. I started hanging out at the health food store, learning how to cook tofu, and buying green powders. I read everything I could about nutrition, herbal medicine, and meditation. It didn't take long before I knew that I would devote my life to supporting others in their wellbeing. I was learning about exciting things called phytochemicals and how chronic stress could be damaging to our health. These new-to-me ideas felt deeply empowering and created a strong desire to understand the incredible potential of the human body.

What I'm describing, of course, is the burgeoning wellness movement, which started out as a relatively well-intentioned—albeit deeply problematic in its cultural appropriation—backlash to dieting and growing rates of chronic disease. Unfortunately, these days wellness looks more like the '90s weight loss it originally opposed than it would ever dare admit. We may have traded fear of fat for fear of carbs, but we still deal in restrictive diets, dubious supplements, and influencers more interested in their metrics than our actual wellbeing. I don't know about you, but it feels like a bit of a circus, and I'm over it.

If wellness doesn't make you feel well, then why the heck are we here? Give me joy! Make it fun! I want to feel *good*. It's time to dial down the noise. I have spent the last few years working to reconnect to my intuition about how to care for myself. I am learning how to feel good in my body as it evolves over time. And more than anything, I just want to have some friends over and eat some wildly delicious food.

Building a Post-Wellness Future

After more than a decade as a dietitian, I find myself at a crossroads. On the one hand, I know the power of feeding yourself well so that you can feel your best. It is a privilege to help guide people toward their healthiest selves—those who might have given up on feeling better, who once again find their spark. On the other hand, I also see the significant harm that a well-intentioned, but often misplaced, focus on wellness media causes the very people who need it most (which, frankly, is all of us). *Plant Magic* is my response to a life lived in wellness and coming out the other side wanting to share what I have learned about what it means to actually take good care of yourself through nutrition.

In the end, it all comes back to plants. I want to show you the sheer joy of cooking and eating plants. In doing so, you'll experience their powerful effect on your body. Humans have looked to plants as partners in our self-care for as long as we have been on this planet. And it is to plants we can return to show us the way forward. Every herb, seed, fruit, and root carries its own unique combination of vitamins, minerals, and, yes, phytochemicals that support our bodies' everyday workings. There is no need to over-complicate things. Mother Nature has our backs.

Cooking is a vital part of this equation because taking the time to cook a simple meal means that you stop letting others decide what goes in your belly. It deepens your connection to food—and to nature itself—as you spend more time in direct contact with the plants you are about to eat. So many of us live in our ideas about what food is—good, bad, super, junk, healthy, unhealthy—and cooking brings us back to a very tangible place of noticing that food is just, well, food.

Positive Nutrition

When you find yourself getting caught up in the wellness doom-scroll, repeat this phrase: pattern over plate. It sounds simple, but taking this advice to heart will liberate you from the minutiae of nutrition. No one food, ingredient, or meal has the power to make or break your health. Instead, it is the overall pattern of how you eat over weeks, months, and years that moves the dial.

So, what does that pattern look like? Yes, it's about getting as many nutrient-dense plants into your body as you can. But it's also recognizing that since forever is a very long time, there is plenty of wiggle room for whatever else you want to eat. Eating well isn't about rigidly following some wacky diet or restricting foods. So take a deep breath and delete that seven-day cleanse from your cart. Tomorrow, try adding an extra serving of vegetables to your dinner. The next day, do it again.

I practise something called positive nutrition, which means that I would rather talk about what to eat more of than about what to avoid. There are two clear advantages to this kind of mindset: the first is that your brain loves the idea of more. As soon as you try to eat less of something, your mind will fight back hard with a nasty case of food preoccupation. But more? That's cozy. That sets your mind at ease. The second advantage is that as much as what you read on the internet would have you believe otherwise, your health is determined by the things you put into your body, not by what you leave out. For example, you can be a sugar-free, gluten-free vegan and not eat a lot of vegetables. It's worth noting that if you really hate the food you are eating in the name of "wellness," it takes a mental and emotional toll that is just as impactful to your wellbeing as anything you're eating.

Another often overlooked component of wellness is food as a source of pleasure in your life, although this is something that our North American culture seems deeply uncomfortable with. On the one hand, we're obsessed with over-the-top indulgence. On the other hand, we are equally obsessed with absolving ourselves of the guilt associated with said indulgence. The infuriating part of this is that both extremes are simply bolstering someone else's bottom line, and they don't actually serve you. News flash: there's no magic eraser for yesterday's dinner, nor does there need to be. And when you let go of labelling foods as good or bad, you start to realize that indulgence can look like chili cheese fries, and it can also look like a perfectly ripe peach, eaten at the height of summer.

The Joy of Eating Plants

Food is more than just an assortment of nutrients. It is a source of comfort, a way of connecting with others and with our culture, and I'll say it again, a source of pleasure. If it's not joyful, I don't want it. If adhering to a way of eating is causing you stress, it's not healthy no matter how "good" it looks on paper. You get to decide what healthy looks like for you. I'm here as a guide, but I am not in your body. Take what resonates and leave the rest.

As someone with a deep love of juicy green smoothies and well-seasoned kale salads, it's not lost on me that one of the unintended consequences of wellness is that we tend to fetishize the "fun stuff" like cake or nachos and associate nutrient-dense plants with deprivation. This is unfair because roasted broccoli is so delicious that I could eat a whole pound of it. Plant foods have an abundance of flavours and textures that are infinitely enjoyable once we drop the idea that healthy eating is plain steamed everything. It is, in fact, possible to feed the body and the soul at the same time.

Lest you think that this comes easy to me because I was a kitchen wunderkind from an early age, you should probably know that the height of my culinary prowess in my twenties was a roughly chopped Greek salad and steamed broccoli on a bed of boxed mac and cheese. If something didn't taste delicious enough, I just added more cheese, three meals a day. Even now, I'm not immune to some epic fails. I'm a self-taught home cook, just like you.

So I know that there is a space between wanting to eat a certain way and having the skills to make it happen. If you're new to plant-based cooking, you may not even know where to start. Maybe you're hoping to feel better, or to minimize your impact on animals or the planet, or simply to eat some yummy plants. Regardless of your why, *Plant Magic* is here for you. As you cook the recipes in these pages, you'll start to notice all my little tricks for coaxing the best out of simple plant foods like beans, grains, and vegetables. Such as how I use garlic and onion powder as umami bombs. Or the way I add a little sugar to a salad dressing to soften any bitterness or overly sour notes. My intention in creating these recipes is to show you how delicious plant-based food can be and that sometimes healthy eating looks like a kale salad and sometimes it looks like tiramisu.

Despite the symphony of strong (and often wrong) opinions on what you should and should not eat, there are very few evidence-based absolutes in nutrition. Why? Because each one of us is unique. We have different bodies, cultural backgrounds, and budgets. We also have different goals, health concerns, and taste buds.

I said there are very few absolutes, which means that, yes, there are a couple of them. Curious? The first is to drink plenty of water. Your body loses a significant amount of water each day, and you need to rehydrate. And the second? Eat as many whole plant foods as you can. That's pretty much it! I would be remiss if I didn't say that our body has a biological requirement for certain nutrients, such as protein, vitamins, and minerals, but eating a variety of foods over the course of a day, or a week, will take care of most of it. There is no one perfect diet. There is no one food that will heal or harm you, aside from legitimate food allergies, of course. It is up to you to choose the way of eating that is right for you, and you don't need to put a label on it. You don't have to be vegan to eat a vegan dinner. You can eat millet because it's delicious and not because it's gluten-free. And you can eat potato chips and still be healthy.

Sound good? Then it's time to start falling in love with plants in all their forms. Before we dive into the recipes, I've included a section on how to make all this plant magic happen for yourself—from getting your pantry stocked to tricks for making delicious meals without meat and dairy. And as you pore through the recipes, you'll notice a few essays on what living well means to me. They're kind of like a side dish of food for thought to go with the actual food. Now, let's eat!

How to Create Plant Magic

My love of cooking was born of my love of eating. Transforming a handful of ingredients into a meal that makes you feel good is the best kind of magic.

But that doesn't mean I always want—or have time—to cook. I know we all have our own relationship with cooking, so rest assured that as much as I hope the recipes in this book will help you love cooking a little more, it's also totally okay to want to do the minimum necessary to enjoy a nourishing, delicious meal. Some of the recipes in this book are perfect for those nights when you're just trying to avoid calling for takeout, while others are more of a settle in and get cozy type of cooking.

Whether you're new to plant-based cooking or just need a little reboot in the kitchen department, this chapter will help teach you the essential ingredients for making magic in the kitchen. Let's start by getting your kitchen ready, and then I'll give you a few tricks and tools to make everything easier—and tastier!

Dial Up Your Plant Pantry

Given that I create about a hundred recipes a year, I'm pretty much always riding the razor-thin edge between having a well-stocked pantry and having way too much of everything. So let me help you not do that!

Gathering an assortment of hard-working staples will make it so much easier to cook for yourself on the fly with whatever's in season, but it's important to be realistic about how often you cook and how many mouths you're feeding. If you're cooking for one, feel free to buy a bit larger on the condiments and spices that make everything delicious but keep a smaller cache of food items, perhaps just two or three each of grains or nuts on hand at any one time, to ensure that you use them up while they're still fresh.

When it comes to fruits and vegetables, do yourself and your wallet a favour by letting what is in season guide you. Seasonal produce tastes much better and typically costs less than having to fly something in out of season. Granted, here in Canada the season is a wee bit shorter than, say, in California, but if you've got a solid pantry, you'll be able to make magic with whatever lands in your cart this week.

Whole Grains. Rolled oats, spelt or wheat berries, rice, quinoa, millet, sprouted grain bread, and noodles.

Flours. Almond flour, gluten-free flour blend, spelt flour, whole wheat flour, and chickpea flour.

Oils + Condiments. Extra-virgin olive oil or avocado oil, coconut oil, soy sauce, tamari, Dijon mustard, white and red miso, apple cider vinegar, balsamic vinegar, rice vinegar, red wine vinegar, hot sauce, and stock concentrate.

Dried Herbs + Spices. Cumin, coriander, smoked paprika, sweet paprika, onion powder, garlic powder, cinnamon, cardamom, oregano, and thyme.

Salt + Pepper. I keep on hand iodized sea salt for cooking and flaky sea salt for finishing.

Proteins. Dried or canned lentils, chickpeas, black beans, and cannellini beans.

Cans + Jars. Kalamata olives, capers, sundried and diced tomatoes, tomato paste, coconut milk, and roasted red peppers.

Flavour Boosters. Lemons, limes, garlic, onions, shallots, and ginger.

Sweets. Cane sugar, brown sugar, dates, maple syrup, vanilla, and dairy-free chocolate chips.

Nuts + Seeds. Hemp hearts, almonds, cashews, chia seeds, ground flaxseed, walnuts, dried coconut, pumpkin seeds, and sunflower seeds.

Butters. Natural peanut butter, tahini, almond butter, and sunflower seed butter.

Coriander

Paprika

Tumeric

Cinnamon

Cumin

Spice World

Cardamom

Fennel

Sumac

Fenugreek

Spices are powerful plants with a longstanding history of use in both cooking and traditional medicine. If you're serious about flavour, it's time to start measuring your spices in spoonfuls, not sprinkles.

Cinnamon (ground and sticks). Amplifies sweet flavours and may support better blood sugar balance when used regularly.

Coriander (ground). The ground seeds of the coriander (or cilantro) plant. Coriander supports digestion and contains a host of phytochemicals such as quercetin.

Cumin (seeds and ground). The spice I use most often, with anti-inflammatory and digestion-soothing properties.

Fennel (seeds and ground). Rich in phytochemicals, try chewing on a few seeds to ease digestion and freshen breath after a meal.

Fenugreek. Mineral rich, fenugreek may support cardiometabolic health.

Paprika (ground). Hot, sweet, or smoky, paprika is made from dried and ground red peppers, rich in capsaicin, and known for analgesic and anti-inflammatory properties.

Sumac (ground). Made from ground sumac berries, lends a citrusy flavour to dishes and may have antimicrobial effects.

Turmeric (ground). An anti-inflammatory all-star, pair turmeric with black pepper and a little fat to aid in absorption.

Heat

Spices

Alliums

Welcome to Flavour City

Acids

Herbs

These are the elements I use most often to build flavour, because salt is not the only game in town!

Acids. Food taste flat? Acids like apple cider vinegar and lemon juice make flavours come alive, brightening an overly earthy note or neutralizing bitterness. Before you add more salt, try a squeeze of lemon and see if that helps!

Alliums. Aside from being highly nutritious and affordable, alliums like garlic, shallots, and onions are the flavour foundation of any good dish, which is why most of my recipes start with at least one. I also use an immodest amount of garlic and onion powder as my not-so-secret strategy for boosting umami.

Heat. Adding heat isn't always about making a food spicy, although I love that too. Adding a pinch of red chili flakes, for example, creates another dimension that lifts the flavour of a dish, much as acids do.

Herbs. Fresh herbs are leafy greens with a ton of flavour. These aromatic plants are generally added at the end of cooking, and most should be measured in handfuls, not spoonfuls.

Spices. I think that spices are the soul of any dish: they create complex flavours in plant-based cooking and ensure that your dinner is anything but bland.

Parsley

Lavender

Rose

Everyday Herbals

Chamomile

Mint

Chamomile. A calming nervine herb that is safe for all ages and has a mild, grassy flavour.

Lavender. Another calming nervine herb, lavender can be brewed as a tea or used to flavour baked goods, but remember that a little goes a long way.

Mint. Invigorating and soothing to the digestive tract, mint makes a cooling tea and is a delicious addition to sauces and salads.

Parsley. The hardest working leafy green in your fridge, with a zesty, energizing flavour and tons of antioxidants.

Rose. Thought to have cooling, calming qualities, unsprayed rose petals are edible and rose water can be used to fragrance drinks and desserts.

How NOT to Let Everything in Your Produce Drawer Rot

I've been a dietitian for a long time, which means I have spent well over a decade helping people figure out how to get more plants on their plate. One constant in all these years? Most of us aren't eating as many fruits and vegetables as we could.

Affordability is a major component, and relying on less expensive staples like carrots, onions (yes, onions are a legit vegetable!), and frozen veggies can really help. But another equally important barrier is that people don't want to see all the produce they bought go bad before they use it. So, let's talk strategies so that you can buy your bushel of kale and eat it too.

1. Store produce properly.

If you've ever had a huge bunch of kale wilt overnight, you know how frustrating it is. It ruins your budget and your meal plan, so let's fix this.

- Keep fruits and vegetables in separate drawers. Many fruits release ethylene gas that causes vegetables to wilt.
- Treat fresh herbs like flowers. Trim the stems, place it in a glass of water in the fridge, and cover with a plastic bag.
- Line packages of prewashed greens with paper towel to absorb the moisture that leads to spoilage.
- For bunches of greens, regulate humidity by wrapping them in paper towel and then placing them in a reusable silicone bag. Your kale will last a week.

2. Plan your meals based on what keeps longest.

- Delicate items like leafy salad greens are best used within a few days, while hardier veggies like beets and carrots will last a week. Out of fresh produce? Enjoy frozen until your next trip to the grocery store.

3. Revive wilted produce.

- A lot of veggies will crisp up if you place them in cold water for a while. Didn't work? Dice and add them to soups, stews, or fried rice. Freeze brown bananas, which are perfect for smoothies. Purée an overage of herbs and freeze them in ice cube trays for easy recipe additions.

The Life-Changing Magic of Freezing Beans

I admit, I'm not much of a meal prepper. I don't like spending my weekend thinking about food, since I spend most of my workweek doing just that. But I do opt for something I call planned leftovers. For example, if I'm going to make a chili, I make a lot. Why? Because then we have lunch for the next day, or I can freeze it for a night when things are too hectic for cooking.

I rarely make just a tiny bit of sauces, long-cooking grains, or beans, because having those things ready in the fridge or freezer makes it easy to pull together meals later on. And yes, I did just suggest you pop beans in the freezer.

As a bean evangelist, I often am asked whether canned or dried beans are healthier for you, and my answer is, "The beans you'll eat are the best beans for you." Which is 100 percent true: the types of nutrients we seek from our leguminous friends—protein, fibre, and minerals—are super stable in the canning process so nothing is lost from this planty fast food. Dried beans do have a couple of advantages, the first being that they literally cost pennies a serving as well as having a nicer texture. Cooking from scratch is much easier than you think, so if you're curious, here's how to do it.

First things first: do *not* cook a handful of beans. If you are going to take the time to soak beans from scratch, do yourself a favour and cook at least a pound of dried beans. Not sure how you'll use all those beans? We'll get to that. For now, just trust me.

Step 1: Soak your beans for at least 8 hours, and up to 24 hours. It's great to do this before you go to bed, so set a reminder in your phone. Do you "have" to soak beans? No, you don't; they'll just take a bit longer to cook. But real talk: soaking them will minimize the indigestible carbohydrates that make beans such a musical fruit. And since most people worry that beans make them too gassy, you might want to listen to the gut health dietitian on this one.

Step 2: Pour off the soaking liquid, rinse the beans well, and then place them in a large pot with enough fresh water to cover them by 3 inches (8 cm). See all that sudsy liquid you're pouring off? Those are the bubbles that would have ended up in your belly. You're welcome.

Step 3: Bring your beans to a boil and let them cook, skimming off the foam as needed, until tender. How long, you ask? Check them at 30 minutes, then every 15 minutes after that. Cooking time will vary with the type and freshness of the beans. No dried beans will be ready in less than 30 minutes, and most will be in the range of 45 to 75 minutes. Lentils, on the other hand, should be checked after 10 minutes—and then watch them like a hawk.

Step 4: What to do with this gargantuan amount of beans you just made? If you know you're going to use some in the next few days, place them in a storage container, covered in some of the cooking liquid. Cool and then pop them into the fridge. You're going to freeze the rest. To prepare, drain the remaining beans in a colander and rinse well with cool water.

Step 5: Line a rimmed baking sheet with parchment paper. Shake as much water from the beans as possible, then spread them onto the baking sheet. Freeze for 2 hours until solid, then transfer to freezer bags. Now you've got fully cooked beans at the ready whenever you need them. They're like canned beans, but homemade. Pop them directly into a soup or stew, or if you need them for a salad or scramble, you can just boil them for 1 minute or soak them in some hot water for 10 minutes to thaw while you prep the rest of your recipe.

Make It Good

Food is more than a checklist of nutrients. In the name of wellness, folks will suffer through bland, flavourless, or downright sludgy things because they believe it's healthier. That ends now.

I strongly believe that you should enjoy what you're eating. If it's not delicious, what's the point? I'm not saying that every single thing you eat has to be a ten on a scale of one to ten. Sometimes you've just got to put some beans on toast and call it a win. That's real life. But for those who say that plant-based cooking lacks flavour, well, it's probably because they're not cooking with flavour in mind.

When people experiment with plant-based cooking, a common strategy is to simply remove the animal products from your plate and call it a day. That ends up biting you in the butt, because those foods were offering both nutrition and flavour that need to be replaced so that you can be truly satisfied by what's on your plate. And creating delicious, satisfying plant-based meals is actually pretty simple, once you know a few tricks. And that's what this chapter is all about, so let's talk about how to build flavourful meals every single time.

A Word about Salt

I'm going to put on my dietitian hat for a minute and tell you that we've got salt all wrong. While it's true that North Americans consume far too much sodium, that's only half the story. What we don't talk about is that most of that sodium comes from prepared and hyper-processed foods—more than 70 percent actually—so if we're consuming mostly whole plant foods, we have a little room in our sodium budget to cook with salt.

The other part of the equation is that whole plant foods offer what hyper-processed and fast foods don't: electrolyte minerals—namely potassium, magnesium, and calcium—that contribute to sodium balance in the body.

It's recommended that we consume no more than 2300 mg of sodium a day, which is roughly 1 teaspoon (5 mL) of salt per person. But before you freak out that a recipe has a teaspoon of salt in it, note how many people it's supposed to serve—you're not eating that whole teaspoon by yourself. Of course, if you've got doctor's orders to eat less salt, reduce salt by half where necessary.

Now, let's talk flavour. Under-salting your food is a one-way ticket to blandsville. If you're already used to low-salt cooking, you can start with less than I do because your taste buds have adjusted and you can always add more. But most of us in North America are used to highly seasoned foods, and embracing that in your plant-based cooking is key to success. As Molly Baz says, when used correctly salt doesn't make food salty, it makes food taste more like itself. So don't skip the advice to salt your vegetables a bit before the rest of the ingredients go in. And at the end of cooking, before you even think about dishing out the recipe, taste it. Love it? Then nothing more is needed. But what if it's kind of meh? Salt it until it tastes effing delicious.

Tools of the Plant Trade

I have a tiny kitchen with very little storage space, so I am the last person to advocate for a lot of kitchen tools. But having the right tools on deck will make cooking a much more enjoyable experience. What can I say, life is compromise!

Bowls

- Most sets of mixing bowls include small (6 cups/1½ quarts), medium (12 cups/3 quarts), and large (20 cups/5 quarts).

Knives

- 8- or 12-inch (20- or 30-cm) chef's knife
- 4-inch (10-cm) paring knife

Baking Sheets, Pots + Pans

- A couple of rimmed half-sheet pans (18 × 13 inches/46 × 33 cm)
- Pots in small, medium, and large
- Large nonstick skillet (it's handy to have a small and medium skillet as well)
- Cast-iron or enamel Dutch oven (if budget permits)
- Small and medium saucepans
- 8-quart (7.5 L) soup pot

Baking Pans + Dishes

- 9 × 5-inch (2 L) loaf pan
- 12-cup muffin tin
- Two 8-inch (1.2 L) round cake pans
- 9-inch (2.5 L) square baking dish
- 13 × 9-inch (3.5 L) baking dish

Small Tools + Equipment

- Box grater
- Composite cutting board (large)
- Citrus reamer

- Colander (large metal colander for straining soaked nuts and pasta)
- Fine-mesh sieve (for straining lentils and dusting)
- Ladle
- Mandoline (nice to have)
- Measuring cups and spoons
- Metal tongs
- Microplane grater
- Parchment paper (to line your baking sheets for quick cleanup)
- Silicone spatula
- Whisk
- Wooden spoons
- Vegetable peeler

Small Appliances

- Bullet blender
- Food processor
- Hand mixer
- High-speed blender
- Immersion blender
- Stand mixer

If I had to choose between a food processor and high-speed blender, I'd choose a blender. However, a food processor does some things better, like blending small volumes of dips or nut butters.

A lot of the recipes in this book require the power of a high-speed blender. It's a worthwhile investment. If you have a bullet blender, it will also get you through many of the recipes, but you'll have to blend in batches. I also have managed incredible feats with a strong immersion blender and nothing more than my stubbornness to guide me.

1 Morning Things

Chocolate Chip Spelt Pancakes

Makes 10 to 12 pancakes
Gluten-Free Option
Low-FODMAP Option
Nut-Free
Vegan

There is no surer route to my children's hearts than to add chocolate to whatever I'm making. Made with nutrient-dense spelt flour, these quick and easy pancakes have a lighter texture than you'd expect and a deeply satisfying flavour. I love making a double batch and freezing the leftovers to enjoy as a midweek treat whenever I need a little boost.

2¼ cups (550 mL) whole-grain spelt or whole wheat flour

2 teaspoons (10 mL) baking powder

½ teaspoon (2 mL) baking soda

½ teaspoon (2 mL) salt

1½ cups (375 mL) unsweetened oat milk

2 tablespoons (30 mL) pure maple syrup, plus more for serving

¼ cup (60 mL) melted vegan butter or avocado oil, plus more for cooking

1 tablespoon (15 mL) freshly squeezed lemon juice or apple cider vinegar

2 teaspoons (10 mL) pure vanilla extract

¼ cup (60 mL) mini dairy-free chocolate chips

Vegan butter, for serving

1. Preheat the oven to 200°F (100°C). Line a baking sheet with parchment paper.

2. In a large bowl, stir together the spelt flour, baking powder, baking soda, and salt.

3. In a small bowl, whisk together the oat milk, maple syrup, melted butter, lemon juice, and vanilla. Add the wet ingredients to the dry ingredients, stir, and let sit for 5 minutes to thicken. Fold in the chocolate chips.

4. Melt 1 tablespoon (15 mL) of the butter in a large nonstick skillet over medium heat. Cooking in batches, pour ⅓ cup (75 mL) of batter into the pan and cook until bubbles appear on the surface of the pancake and the edges look cooked, 2 to 4 minutes. Flip and cook for another 2 to 4 minutes, until golden brown on the bottom. Transfer to the prepared baking sheet and keep warm in the oven while you cook the remaining pancakes.

5. Serve the pancakes with maple syrup and a pat of butter. Freeze leftover pancakes on a baking sheet lined with parchment paper until frozen. Then transfer to a resealable freezer bag and store in the freezer for up to 2 weeks. Reheat from frozen in the toaster.

Swaps + Stuff
For a gluten-free and low-FODMAP option, swap a legume-free, starch-based gluten-free flour blend, such as Bob's Red Mill Gluten Free 1-to-1 Baking Flour, for the spelt or whole wheat flour.

Brownie Batter Breakfast Toast

Makes about 1½ cups (375 mL) spread

Gluten-Free Option
Low-FODMAP Option
Nut-Free
Vegan

I was one of those kids who grew up thinking it was as normal to spread chocolate on your morning toast as it was peanut butter. So, creating a Nutella-like chocolate spread has been on my mind for a while. This dreamy chocolate spread is so creamy and rich, you'll never guess that it packs a ton of essential omega-3 fatty acids and protein from hemp hearts. The next time someone asks if you take omega-3s, tell them you're covered, in the form of this too good to be true spread slathered over whole-grain toast. Or try it as a fruit dip or even as frosting on a cake.

1¼ cups (300 mL) hemp hearts

¼ cup (60 mL) raw cacao powder or cocoa powder

⅓ cup (75 mL) pure maple syrup

3 tablespoons (45 mL) avocado oil

3 tablespoons (45 mL) water

2 teaspoons (10 mL) pure vanilla extract

¼ teaspoon (1 mL) salt

Whole-grain or gluten-free bread, toasted, for serving

1. In a small blender or bullet blender, combine the hemp hearts, cacao powder, maple syrup, avocado oil, water, vanilla, and salt. Starting on low speed and slowly increasing to medium, blend until smooth, 4 to 5 minutes. (If using a large blender jar, you'll have to stop the blender and scrape down the sides of the bowl a few times; however, a smooth spread will form with almost no trace of hemp seed.)

2. Spread generously on toast. Store the spread in an airtight container in the fridge for up to 1 week.

Swaps + Stuff

The spread is gluten-free. Use gluten-free bread if required.

For a low-FODMAP serving, use 2 tablespoons (30 mL) of spread and gluten-free bread.

After Eight Smoothie

Serves 1

Gluten-Free

Low-FODMAP Option

Nut-Free Option

Vegan

I will forever associate the pairing of chocolate and mint with sneaking more than my fair share as a child from the boxes of holiday chocolates that were scattered around the house. This smoothie recreates that nostalgic and comforting flavour because, in my opinion, it's never too early in the day for chocolate. The comforting nature of this smoothie goes beyond nostalgia: cocoa contains a molecule called anandamide, thought to make it a good-mood food, while the peppermint helps soothe fussy digestive tracts.

1 cup (250 mL) unsweetened almond or macadamia milk

1 ripe medium banana

A handful of baby spinach

2 tablespoons (30 mL) hemp hearts

2 tablespoons (30 mL) cocoa powder or raw cacao powder

1 teaspoon (5 mL) pure mint extract (or ¼ teaspoon/1 mL pure peppermint culinary oil)

1 scoop chocolate or vanilla vegan protein powder

1 cup (250 mL) ice cubes

1 tablespoon (15 mL) pure maple syrup (optional)

1 tablespoon (15 mL) raw cacao nibs (optional)

1. In a high-speed blender, combine the almond milk, banana, spinach, hemp hearts, cocoa powder, mint extract, protein powder, ice cubes, and maple syrup, if using. Blend until smooth. Add the cacao nibs (if using) and blend for another 10 seconds to break them up a bit. Pour into a glass.

Swaps + Stuff

For a nut-free version, swap oat milk for the nut milk.

For a low-FODMAP version, use a low-FODMAP protein powder, such as rice protein powder, and use a third of a banana.

Blackberry Basil Smoothie

Makes 2 snack-size servings

Gluten-Free

Nut-Free Option

Vegan

This delicious smoothie, bursting with juicy flavour, is the perfect balance of sweet berries and vanilla, herbaceous notes from the basil, and earthy tahini. High in fibre for a healthier gut, blackberries are as delicious as they are nourishing, packed with phytochemicals that help fight oxidative damage and inflammation, as well as vitamin C. This smoothie is lovely alongside a serving of Brownie Batter Breakfast Toast (page 31). Enjoying this smoothie as a stand-alone breakfast? Swap soy milk for the nut milk or add some protein powder for extra protein to help you feel full and satisfied.

1½ cups (375 mL) fresh or frozen blackberries

1¼ cups (300 mL) unsweetened almond or macadamia milk

1 fresh or frozen ripe medium banana

A handful of spinach

4 large fresh basil leaves

Zest of ¼ lemon

1 tablespoon (15 mL) tahini

1 tablespoon (15 mL) pure vanilla extract

1 tablespoon (15 mL) pure maple syrup (or 1 Medjool date, pitted)

1 cup (250 mL) ice cubes, if not using frozen fruit

Pinch of salt

1. In a high-speed blender, combine the blackberries, almond milk, banana, spinach, basil, lemon zest, tahini, vanilla, maple syrup, ice cubes (if not using frozen fruit), and salt. Blend until smooth. Pour into glasses.

Note: If using all frozen fruit, you'll get more of a smoothie bowl texture. Add more milk to thin as needed to achieve desired texture. This smoothie also makes excellent ice pops. Just pour the smoothie into ice-pop moulds and store in the freezer for up to 1 month.

Swaps + Stuff

For a nut-free version, swap oat milk for the nut milk.

Walnut Apple Breakfast Buckwheat

Serves 2
Gluten-Free
Low-FODMAP Option
Nut-Free Option
Vegan

1 cup (250 mL) buckwheat groats, soaked in water overnight, drained, and rinsed

1 cup (250 mL) water

1 teaspoon (5 mL) cinnamon

⅛ teaspoon (0.5 mL) salt

1 Gala or Honeycrisp apple, cored and diced

½ cup (125 mL) unsweetened soy or oat milk

¼ cup (60 mL) chopped raw walnuts or sunflower seeds

2 tablespoons (30 mL) pure maple syrup

Oats are not the only game in town: buckwheat makes a delicious morning meal. Incredibly nutritious, buckwheat is high in energizing minerals as well as fibre, and its rich, nutty flavour is deeply satisfying. With its texture somewhere between a tender cooked grain and a porridge, I love the crunch of walnuts and apple as a counterpoint to the tender buckwheat, but this would be delicious with any fruit you have on hand, such as bananas, pears, or blueberries.

1. In a small pot, combine the drained buckwheat groats, water, cinnamon, and salt over medium heat. Bring to a boil, then reduce the heat to medium-low and cook, covered with the lid slightly ajar, stirring occasionally, until the buckwheat is tender, 6 to 8 minutes.

2. Stir in the apple, soy milk, walnuts, and maple syrup. Divide between bowls and serve. Store leftovers in an airtight container in the fridge for up to 2 days. Reheat with a bit of warm water over medium heat until steaming.

Swaps + Stuff

For a nut-free version, use raw sunflower seeds instead of walnuts.

For a low-FODMAP version, swap the apple for 5 hulled and sliced strawberries.

How to Be Well without Making Wellness Your Job

What does wellness look like? You might expect me to say that it looks like eating five cups of vegetables a day, working out every day, or ditching sugar. If so, you're going to be surprised by what I say next, because the most important determinants of health aren't individual actions. If we're lucky enough to have access to housing, clean drinking water, safe communities, and health care, it can be easy to forget that without them, it's extremely difficult to be well.

When I imagine wellness, it's not even about being free of a chronic condition like diabetes or celiac disease. In fact, that kind of mindset does a serious disservice to the millions of us that live with these conditions every single day. You can have diabetes, keep your blood sugars in check, and be super active. You can have zero chronic diseases and still feel awful.

I know you're looking for answers and secretly hoping I'm going to tell you that there's a single supplement you can take to fix everything. I'm not evading the question, but I am trying to set you up for the vibe shift: if you want to know if you're truly well, it's time to let how you're feeling be your guide.

How are your energy levels? How is your mood? Do you feel at home in your body, or is it giving you a bit of trouble? Did you eat your vegetables today? Did you spend all day connected to screens, or did you take time for a hike, to read a book, or to snuggle a loved one or a pet? Are you stressed?

Because although wellness is often sold as some glittery Valhalla entered through the doors of an infrared sauna, wellness is not actually an end goal. True wellness is a practice that adapts in response to how you are feeling and your current circumstances. And sometimes what we need most has nothing to do with nutrition. We're not going to feel 100 percent all the time. Sniffles happen. So do crushing deadlines. For me, wellness looks like doing our best to care for ourselves every single day. Some days, that might include a home-cooked meal and a yoga class. Other days, it might be a cozy blanket and Netflix.

What we think of as wellness—adaptogens, grain-free granola, workouts, kombucha—are really just the luxury add-ons. These things can be fun, and some might even be helpful, but they aren't what's driving your wellbeing. They're the sprinkles, not the sundae. In fact, the pillars of self-care are something else entirely, and while they may not be as alluring and well marketed, they are deeply transformative. These are what I consider the pillars of wellness:

Rest

Sleep is an essential time of growth and repair, but it seems we'd rather spend hundreds of dollars on energy supplements than do the work required to get seven to nine hours of sleep a night. Yep, you read that right! As a parent of two, I'm not going to lie and tell you that this is always achievable, but it's more achievable than you think with a few good sleep habits. This means sticking to a regular bedtime. Putting your phone away early so your mind can wind down. Enjoying a relaxing herbal tea, taking a bath, or doing a body scan, whatever ritual you need to welcome sleep.

We also need to talk about the other component of rest that happens when you're awake. As the queen of tired and wired, this one has been a challenge for me. Building rest into your day means maintaining firm boundaries so as not to overextend yourself. If you're working two jobs, maybe you don't need to be the one chairing the school's fundraising committee. It's putting the phone away so that your mind can wander. It's recognizing that you should not be productive twenty-four hours a day and that it's okay to just sit on a bench outdoors and take in the view. When you think about it, rest is a radical act. If you need further nudging, read *Rest Is Resistance* by Tricia Hersey, founder of Nap Ministry.

Drink Water

You live in a fluid medium: every time you perspire, exhale, or excrete, water is lost and you need to replace it. Troubles with fatigue or digestive issues? Maybe it's dehydration. I'm lucky to live in a city with one of the cleanest water supplies in the world, and I drink water straight out of the tap. If you aren't so lucky, get a basic water filter and then get that water into your bod. Your daily water needs are a moving target based on your diet and activity levels, temperature, and humidity. So, how do you know if you're hydrated? If you're going to the bathroom every two to three hours and your urine is pale in colour, then you're hydrated. I try to start my day with 2 cups (500 mL) of water and then I keep a large bottle of water at my side so that I have a visual cue to sip often. It's infuriating to think that, even in North America, not everyone has access to clean drinking water. Just in case you're wondering, wellness is also advocacy.

Eat Some Plants

If you have the privilege of enough food to eat, start by putting more plants on your plate. You don't need to count things or follow any special diet unless it's medically required for a health condition. Just look for opportunities to eat whole plant foods. Grab an apple or a handful of cashews as a snack. Make a smoothie. Dunk crackers into an eggplant dip. Make a lentil stew. For many of us, it really is that simple. Need a spot check? The easiest check for balanced nutrition is the plate method: whenever possible, make half your plate fruit and vegetables, a quarter of your plate whole grains or starchy veggies, and a quarter of your plate protein-rich plants like legumes, tofu, or tempeh. Not every meal needs to look like this; sometimes I just want a big old bowl of pasta. Remember, pattern over plate.

Move

If your body moves, move it. Movement is our natural state and supports not just our physical wellbeing but also our mental wellbeing. I am a much happier person after a good sweat. Many of us sit all day, and the power of getting that blood and lymph pumping through your body is immense. It doesn't matter what you do as long as it's something you enjoy so you'll actually keep doing it. Fancy classes can be fun and motivating, but movement can also be as simple as biking to work, taking a sweaty brisk walk, or doing a YouTube yoga session.

If you're noticing just how simple this advice is, remember that simple and easy are not the same thing. An entire wellness ecosystem has been built to try to make us feel better because we are not actually living in accordance with these pillars; so why not just get back to basics? You might be surprised by how good you feel. And another thing: wellness is meant for all of us. If you have a body, it wants to be well. Free yourself from other people's ideas of what wellness is—which may serve them and not you. You know your body best, and only you can determine what wellness looks like for you.

Baked Oats for All Seasons

Serves 6
Gluten-Free Option
Low-FODMAP Option
Vegan

Whenever I can set it and forget it, I will. With minimal hands-on time, baked oats are a nice change from everyday oatmeal because you can pop them in the oven when you wake up and they'll be ready when you are. Fragrant with ripe persimmons and cardamom, these baked oats are comforting, cozy, and incredibly nourishing on a cold winter's day. I like a little drizzle of almond milk on top. And when persimmon season is over, I have variations to carry you through the rest of the year (see below).

2½ cups (625 mL) old-fashioned rolled oats

½ cup (125 mL) hemp hearts

¼ cup (60 mL) ground flaxseed

1 teaspoon (5 mL) baking powder

1 teaspoon (5 mL) ground cardamom

½ teaspoon (2 mL) cinnamon

½ teaspoon (2 mL) salt

¼ cup (60 mL) cashew or almond butter

½ cup (125 mL) pure maple syrup

2½ cups (625 mL) unsweetened almond milk

2 ripe Fuyu persimmons, diced

¼ cup (60 mL) chopped raw hazelnuts or almonds

1. Preheat the oven to 350°F (180°C). Line a 9-inch (2.5 L) square baking dish with parchment paper.

2. In a large bowl, stir together the rolled oats, hemp hearts, flaxseed, baking powder, cardamom, cinnamon, and salt.

3. In a medium bowl, whisk together the cashew butter and maple syrup (this will loosen up the cashew butter a bit). Pour in the almond milk and whisk until smooth. Add the wet ingredients to the dry ingredients and stir until fully combined. Fold in the persimmon and hazelnuts. Pour the mixture into the prepared baking dish.

4. Bake until set in the middle, 45 to 50 minutes. Remove from the oven and let cool for 10 minutes before serving. Store, covered, on the counter for up to 1 day or in the fridge for up to 3 days.

Swaps + Stuff

For a gluten-free version, use gluten-free rolled oats.

For a low-FODMAP version, use almond butter instead of cashew butter and 2 cups (500 mL) of strawberries and ¼ cup (60 mL) of chopped raw almonds as the flavour variation.

Seasonal Variations

Spring: Swap 2 ripe bananas, sliced into rounds, and ¼ cup (60 mL) dried unsweetened coconut for the persimmon and nuts.

Summer: Swap 2 cups (500 mL) mixed fresh berries and ¼ cup (60 mL) chopped or slivered raw almonds for the persimmon and nuts.

Fall: Swap 2 cups (500 mL) chopped apple and ¼ cup (60 mL) chopped raw walnuts for the persimmon and nuts.

Blueberry Coconut Breakfast Cookies

Makes 15 cookies
Gluten-Free
Low-FODMAP Option
Nut-Free Option
Vegan

Are breakfast cookies a personality trait? If so, I'll happily claim it as mine. These just might be the best breakfast cookies I've ever created. A hint of lemon, luscious blueberries, and creamy cashew butter make these cookies satisfying to the stomach and the soul. Waking up slowly with a cup of tea and one of these cookies is the best way to start the day. Of course, not all mornings are as idyllic but, rest assured, these cookies are the perfect grab-and-go breakfast when time is tight.

1½ cups (375 mL) gluten-free old-fashioned rolled oats

1½ cups (375 mL) unsweetened shredded coconut

2 tablespoons (30 mL) ground flaxseed

1 teaspoon (5 mL) baking powder

½ teaspoon (2 mL) cinnamon

½ teaspoon (2 mL) salt

Zest of ½ lemon

2 mashed ripe medium bananas

½ cup (125 mL) cashew butter

3 tablespoons (45 mL) pure maple syrup

1 teaspoon (5 mL) pure vanilla extract

¾ cup (175 mL) fresh or frozen blueberries

Swaps + Stuff

For a nut-free version, swap sunflower seed butter for the cashew butter.

For a low-FODMAP version, swap almond butter for the cashew butter; one cookie is a low-FODMAP serving.

1. Preheat the oven to 375°F (190°C). Line a large baking sheet with parchment paper.

2. In a large bowl, stir together the rolled oats, coconut, flaxseed, baking powder, cinnamon, salt, and lemon zest.

3. In a small bowl, whisk together the mashed banana, cashew butter, maple syrup, and vanilla. Add the wet ingredients to the dry ingredients and begin mixing with a fork. This is a very thick batter, so I recommend using wet hands to finish mixing the batter until no dry patches remain. Gently fold in the blueberries.

4. Working with wet hands (the batter is sticky), scoop ¼ cup (60 mL) of batter and pat into 2-inch (5 cm) rounds. Pack and compress the rounds a bit to keep the blueberries in place. Arrange the cookies on the prepared baking sheet, evenly spaced. If the batter starts to stick to your hands, simply rinse it off with water and keep working with wet hands. Bake until the cookies are golden brown on the bottom and browning around the top edges, 17 to 19 minutes. Let the cookies cool completely on the baking sheet to firm up. Store in a loosely covered container on the counter for up to 3 days or in an airtight container in the fridge for up to 1 week or in the freezer for up to 1 month.

Blueberry Sweet Corn Muffins

Makes 12 muffins

Nut-Free

Vegan

1¾ cups (425 mL) whole-grain spelt or whole wheat flour

¾ cup (175 mL) fine cornmeal

1 teaspoon (5 mL) baking powder

1 teaspoon (5 mL) baking soda

½ teaspoon (2 mL) salt

¼ teaspoon (1 mL) cinnamon

1 cup (250 mL) unsweetened oat or soy milk

½ cup (125 mL) unsweetened applesauce

½ cup (125 mL) cane sugar

¼ cup (60 mL) avocado oil

1 tablespoon (15 mL) ground flaxseed

1 tablespoon (15 mL) apple cider vinegar

1 tablespoon (15 mL) pure vanilla extract

½ cup (125 mL) fresh or thawed frozen blueberries

½ cup (125 mL) canned or fresh sweet corn kernels, cooked and cooled (see Note)

Yes, I put sweet corn in muffins. And yes, it's delicious. Blueberries and corn are a classic pairing that puts me in a summer state of mind, no matter how terrible the weather is outside. These just-sweet-enough muffins have a deeply satisfying yet not too dense texture thanks to whole-grain spelt flour and fine cornmeal. Wonderful for breakfast, snack time, or anytime you need a little sunshine on your plate.

1. Preheat the oven to 375°F (190°C). Line a 12-cup muffin tin with paper liners.

2. In a large bowl, stir together the spelt flour, cornmeal, baking powder, baking soda, salt, and cinnamon.

3. In a medium bowl, whisk together the oat milk, applesauce, sugar, avocado oil, flaxseed, apple cider vinegar, and vanilla. Add the wet ingredients to the dry ingredients and stir until just combined. Gently fold in the blueberries and corn.

4. Scoop ⅓ cup (75 mL) of batter into each muffin cup. Bake until a skewer inserted in the centre of a muffin comes out clean and the muffins are golden, 18 to 22 minutes. Let the muffins cool in the tin for 10 minutes, then turn out onto a rack to cool completely. Store in a loosely covered container on the counter for up to 4 days.

Note: If you don't have leftover cooked corn kernels on hand, place the kernels in a small saucepan with 2 table-spoons (30 mL) of water and cook over medium heat for 1 to 2 minutes. This cooks off the starch and enhances sweetness. Drain and use.

Earl Grey Breakfast Loaf

Makes 1 loaf

Nut-Free

Vegan

As far as life hacks go, caffeinating your breakfast is at least on par with prepping your lunches on Sundays or meditating on your morning commute. This moist and delicious breakfast loaf is delicately scented with Earl Grey tea and orange zest and perfect as part of a brunch spread or kept on the counter for whenever the hangries strike. The crunchy streusel layer adds just a bit of decadence.

Streusel Topping

⅓ cup (75 mL) whole-grain spelt or whole wheat flour

¼ cup (60 mL) lightly packed brown sugar

2 tablespoons (30 mL) cold vegan butter

½ teaspoon (2 mL) Earl Grey tea leaves

Zest of ½ orange

⅛ teaspoon (0.5 mL) salt

Breakfast Loaf

2½ cups (625 mL) whole-grain spelt or whole wheat flour

⅓ cup (75 mL) ground flaxseed

1 tablespoon (15 mL) Early Grey tea leaves

1 teaspoon (5 mL) baking powder

1 teaspoon (5 mL) baking soda

½ teaspoon (2 mL) salt

Zest of ½ orange

1 cup (250 mL) unsweetened oat or soy milk

½ cup (125 mL) extra-virgin olive oil, plus more for greasing the pan

½ cup (125 mL) cane sugar

½ cup (125 mL) unsweetened applesauce

3 tablespoons (45 mL) freshly squeezed lemon juice

1 teaspoon (5 mL) pure vanilla extract

1. Preheat the oven to 400°F (200°C). Lightly grease a 9 × 5-inch (2 L) loaf pan with olive oil. Line the pan with parchment paper with extra hanging over the sides.

2. **Make the streusel topping:** In a small bowl, combine the spelt flour, brown sugar, butter, tea leaves, orange zest, and salt. Mix with a fork until it resembles sandy crumbles. Place in the fridge, uncovered, until ready to use.

3. **Make the breakfast loaf:** In a large bowl, stir together the spelt flour, flaxseed, tea leaves, baking powder, baking soda, salt, and orange zest.

4. In a small bowl, whisk together the oat milk, olive oil, sugar, applesauce, lemon juice, and vanilla. Add the wet ingredients to the dry ingredients and stir until just combined. Scrape the batter into the prepared loaf pan. Evenly sprinkle the streusel over the batter.

5. Place the loaf pan on the middle rack of the oven and bake until a skewer inserted in the centre of the loaf comes out clean and the streusel topping is golden, 38 to 42 minutes. Let the loaf cool in the pan for 10 minutes, then carefully lift it onto a rack using the parchment paper overhang. Let cool completely. Using a serrated knife, slice the loaf into 1-inch (2.5 cm) thick slices. Store in a loosely covered container on the counter for up to 3 days or tightly wrapped in the freezer for up to 1 month.

Tahini Caramel Apple Muffins

Makes 12 muffins

Gluten-Free

Nut-Free

Vegan

My love of salt runs deep. I don't know of any food that isn't made more delectable by adding just a bit of salt. After you try these tender apple muffins, topped with a drizzle of salted tahini caramel, I'm sure you'll be on team salted caramel too. You might even find yourself making a double batch of the sauce because you want more than just a drizzle! Be sure to dice the apple into small pieces, as with most gluten-free vegan baking, large pieces can interfere with the structure of the muffin.

Muffins

1½ cups (375 mL) gluten-free all-purpose flour blend (see Note)

1 cup (250 mL) gluten-free old-fashioned rolled oats

¼ cup (60 mL) ground flaxseed

1 teaspoon (5 mL) cinnamon

1 teaspoon (5 mL) baking powder

½ teaspoon (2 mL) baking soda

½ teaspoon (2 mL) salt

1 cup (250 mL) unsweetened applesauce

½ cup (125 mL) avocado oil

½ cup (125 mL) pure maple syrup

1 tablespoon (15 mL) apple cider vinegar

1 tablespoon (15 mL) pure vanilla extract

1 medium Gala or Honeycrisp apple, cored, peeled, and diced

Tahini Caramel Sauce

3 tablespoons (45 mL) pure maple syrup

1 tablespoon (15 mL) vegan butter or coconut oil

1 tablespoon (15 mL) tahini

1 teaspoon (5 mL) pure vanilla extract

¼ teaspoon (1 mL) salt

1. **Make the muffins:** Preheat the oven to 375°F (190°C). Line a 12-cup muffin tin with paper liners.

2. In a large bowl, stir together the gluten-free flour, rolled oats, flaxseed, cinnamon, baking powder, baking soda, and salt.

3. In a small bowl, whisk together the applesauce, avocado oil, maple syrup, apple cider vinegar, and vanilla. Add the wet ingredients to the dry ingredients and stir until well combined. Fold in the apple.

4. Scoop ⅓ cup (75 mL) of batter into each muffin cup. Bake until a skewer inserted into the centre of a muffin comes out clean and the edges are golden brown, 22 to 24 minutes. Let the muffins cool in the tin for 10 minutes, then turn out onto a rack to cool completely.

5. **Once the muffins are cool, make the tahini caramel sauce:** In a small saucepan, combine the maple syrup, butter, tahini, vanilla, and salt over medium heat, and cook, whisking frequently, until the sauce thickens a bit, 1 to 2 minutes. Remove from the heat and let cool to thicken further.

recipe continues

6. Drizzle 1 teaspoon (5 mL) of sauce over each muffin and serve. Store covered on the counter for up to 3 days. The muffins will absorb the caramel over time, decreasing the intensity of flavour. (Alternatively, store the muffins without the sauce, and store the sauce separately in an airtight container in the fridge for up to 4 days. Let the sauce come to room temperature before using for a more spreadable texture.)

Note: I use Bob's Red Mill chickpea-based (not 100% chickpea) Gluten Free All-Purpose Baking Flour, not its Gluten Free 1-to-1 Baking Flour.

Chickpea Frittata with Herby Salad

Serves 4

Gluten-Free

Nut-Free

Vegan

For years before I went plant-based, a frittata was a weekly staple because it was a quick way to get dinner on the table, no matter what I had lurking in the fridge. After experimenting with a bunch of variations, this simple chickpea flour-based version has come out the clear winner. Long used in South Asian cuisine, chickpea flour makes a beautiful replacement for eggs because it is packed with filling protein, fibre, and important minerals. Deeply savoury, with a creamy texture, this not-a-frittata will lend itself easily to as many variations as you can dream up.

Chickpea Frittata

2 cups (500 mL) chickpea flour

1½ cups (375 mL) water

3 tablespoons (45 mL) avocado oil, divided

1½ teaspoons (7 mL) salt

½ teaspoon (2 mL) garlic powder

¼ teaspoon (1 mL) ground turmeric

¼ teaspoon (1 mL) ground coriander

¼ teaspoon (1 mL) baking powder

2 cups (500 mL) bite-size broccoli florets

1 small shallot, finely chopped

1 cup (250 mL) frozen peas

½ teaspoon (2 mL) sweet paprika

¼ teaspoon (1 mL) ground coriander

⅛ teaspoon (0.5 mL) salt

Freshly cracked black pepper

¼ cup (60 mL) vegan feta or Parmesan cheese (optional)

1. **Make the chickpea frittata:** Preheat the oven to 350°F (180°C).

2. In a large bowl, whisk together the chickpea flour, water, 1 tablespoon (15 mL) of the avocado oil, salt, garlic powder, turmeric, coriander, and baking powder. Set aside to let the flour hydrate while you cook the veggies.

3. Heat 1 tablespoon (15 mL) of the avocado oil in a heat-resistant medium nonstick skillet over medium heat. Add the broccoli, shallot, and peas and cook, stirring occasionally, until the broccoli is bright green and the shallot is soft and translucent, 5 to 7 minutes. Add the sweet paprika, coriander, salt, and pepper to taste, and stir. Remove from the heat and let cool for 1 minute. Add the vegetable mixture to the chickpea batter. Sprinkle in the cheese (if using) and stir to combine, ensuring that the vegetables are evenly coated with batter. Wipe the pan.

4. In the same pan, heat the remaining 1 tablespoon (15 mL) avocado oil over medium heat. Pour in the frittata mixture and tilt or swirl the pan to evenly distribute the vegetables. Transfer to the oven and bake until the frittata is dry to the touch on top and starting to crack around the edges, 25 to 30 minutes. The frittata won't brown. Remove from the oven and let sit for 10 minutes.

recipe and ingredients continue

Herby Salad

4 cups (1 L) lightly packed
    arugula

1 cup (250 mL) mixed fresh herbs
    (basil, mint, dill, parsley),
    thinly sliced

1 teaspoon (5 mL) freshly
    squeezed lemon juice

1 teaspoon (5 mL) avocado or
    extra-virgin olive oil

Flaky sea salt

5. Meanwhile, make the herby salad: In a medium bowl, toss together the arugula and fresh herbs with the lemon juice and avocado oil. Season with flaky sea salt to taste.

6. To serve, cut the frittata into wedges and transfer to plates. Top the frittata with some herby salad. Store the frittata, without the salad, in an airtight container in the fridge for up to 3 days. It makes an excellent sandwich filling.

2 Dressed-Up Veg

Garlic-Sautéed Rapini with Creamy Celeriac Mash

If you've ever strolled right on past the knobby, hairy masses of celery root, also known as celeriac, in the produce section, I don't blame you. But I also don't want you to miss out! Once you peel this odd-looking veg, you'll be rewarded with a versatile root that you can turn into a creamy, garlic-flecked mash that is the perfect cozy bed for the almost bracing bitterness of rapini.

Serves 4

Gluten-Free

Nut-Free

Vegan

Creamy Celeriac Mash

1 small celeriac (¾ to 1 pound/340 to 450 g), peeled and cut into 1-inch (2.5 cm) cubes

1½ teaspoons (7 mL) salt, divided

1 clove garlic, peeled

1 can (14 ounces/398 mL) white beans (I like cannellini or navy)

¼ cup (60 mL) unsweetened oat milk

1 tablespoon (15 mL) vegan butter or extra-virgin olive oil

1 tablespoon (15 mL) pure maple syrup

1 teaspoon (5 mL) garlic powder

Freshly cracked black pepper

Garlic-Sautéed Rapini

2 tablespoons (30 mL) extra-virgin olive oil

1 pound (450 g) rapini, ends trimmed (see Note)

2 cloves garlic, finely chopped

Salt

Pinch of red chili flakes

Squeeze of lemon juice

1. **Make the creamy celeriac mash:** Bring a medium pot of water to a boil over high heat. Add the celeriac, 1 teaspoon (5 mL) of the salt, and the garlic. Boil, uncovered, until the celeriac is fork-tender, 10 to 14 minutes. Drain and let cool for 5 minutes.

2. Transfer the celeriac and garlic to a food processor. Add the beans, oat milk, butter, maple syrup, garlic powder, the remaining ½ teaspoon (2 mL) salt, and pepper. Blend until smooth. Set aside.

3. **Make the garlic-sautéed rapini:** Heat the olive oil in a large skillet over medium heat. Place the rapini in the skillet, cover with a lid, and cook for 3 minutes. Remove the lid, add the garlic, and cook, stirring frequently, until the rapini is al dente, 2 to 4 minutes. Remove from the heat. Season well with salt, chili flakes, and a generous squeeze of lemon juice.

4. To serve, spread the creamy celeriac mash on a serving platter or shallow serving bowl. Pile the rapini on top of the mash. Store leftovers in an airtight container in the fridge for up to 3 days.

Note: Rapini is a notably bitter vegetable. If you're new to it, you may enjoy an extra drizzle of maple syrup on top to help your tastebuds adjust. Broccolini or gai lan can be swapped for the rapini.

Grilled Corn with **Roasted Red Pepper Relish**

Serves 6

Gluten-Free

Nut-Free

Vegan

6 sweet corn cobs, shucked

Avocado oil, for brushing and grilling

Roasted Red Pepper Relish (page 294)

Flaky sea salt and freshly cracked black pepper

Summer is generous with her gifts, like lazy days with the sound of waves crashing in your ears, and biting into a cob of sweet, crunchy corn, preferably while the sun shines on your face. Placed on the grill until the kernels are a bit charred, and lavished with a juicy, smoky roasted red pepper relish, corn takes on another, more complex personality that is every bit as enticing. Not that you needed it, but this recipe will give you another excuse to hit the farmers' market and buy an armload of summer-fresh corn while the sun shines.

1. Preheat the grill to medium-high heat (about 500°F/260°C).

2. Brush the corn with avocado oil. Place the corn on the hot grill, close the lid, and grill until nicely charred on all sides, 6 to 8 minutes, turning often. Brush with a bit of roasted red pepper relish on all sides and let cook for 2 more minutes. Transfer to a platter.

3. Sprinkle the grilled corn with flaky sea salt and pepper to taste and spoon more relish over top. Store leftover corn in an airtight container in the fridge for up to 2 days (I like to cut the corn kernels off the cob before storing.)

Swiss Chard Goma-ae

Serves 4

Gluten-Free Option

Low-FODMAP

Nut-Free

Vegan

Before plant-based eating was a thing, a young, newly vegetarian me spent a lot of time in Japan. It was the late '90s and vegetarian food was not super common, which meant I ate a lot of cucumber rolls and goma-ae, a cooked spinach salad dressed in a slightly sweet soy and sesame sauce. It's still one of my favourite ways to eat spinach, but since my garden was exploding with rainbow Swiss chard, I thought I would try giving it the goma-ae treatment and haven't looked back. It's quite simple to make and I've included the stalks as part of the salad to minimize waste, but if you prefer, you can simply reserve them for use in a stew or stir-fry later.

⅓ cup (75 mL) raw sesame seeds

1 pound (450 g) Swiss chard, centre stalks and leaves separated

2 tablespoons (30 mL) soy sauce or gluten-free tamari

2 tablespoons (30 mL) pure maple syrup

2 tablespoons (30 mL) water

Pinch of salt

1. **Toast the sesame seeds:** Heat a small dry skillet over medium heat. Add the sesame seeds and toast, stirring constantly, until golden and fragrant, 5 to 6 minutes. Transfer to a small plate and set aside to cool.

2. **Prepare the Swiss chard:** Cut the Swiss chard stalks into thin 2-inch (5 cm) long matchsticks. Cut the leaves in half lengthwise.

3. Bring a large pot of salted water to a boil over high heat. Carefully drop the chard stems in the boiling water and blanch for 1 minute. Add the leaves and blanch for another 1 minute. Drain in a colander. Rinse the chard under cold running water for 30 seconds to stop the cooking process. Pick out the leaves and firmly squeeze out excess water. Arrange all the leaves lengthwise in one bundle, pat dry with a clean kitchen towel, and cut into 1-inch (2.5 cm) pieces. Set aside. Pat the stems dry and set aside.

4. **Prepare the dressing:** You can use a mortar and pestle, which is the traditional method, or a clean coffee grinder (used only for grinding seeds and spices) to grind the sesame seeds.

recipe continues

If using a mortar and pestle, coarsely grind the sesame seeds (you want a few whole seeds remaining). Add the soy sauce and maple syrup and blend to form a sauce. Thin with the water and add the salt.

If using a coffee grinder, grind half the sesame seeds with 2 or 3 pulses until mostly ground. Transfer to a small bowl. Grind the remaining sesame seeds and transfer to the bowl. Mix in the soy sauce, maple syrup, water, and salt.

5. In a medium bowl, combine the chard stems and leaves and sesame dressing. Toss to coat thoroughly. Store leftovers in an airtight container in the fridge for up to 2 days. Swiss chard goma-ae is a wonderful addition to a rice bowl or snack plate.

Swaps + Stuff

For a gluten-free version, use gluten-free tamari.

Coffee-Roasted Carrots and Crispy Lentils

Serves 4

Gluten-Free

Nut-Free

Vegan

Looking to dress up your usual roasted carrots? How about using coffee with its slight bitterness and aromatics that are a moody counterpoint to sweet maple syrup and bright carrots? If you have never roasted lentils, then you're in for a treat. Not only do they add a boost of fibre and protein, but their crunch adds another layer of texture that makes this dish a satisfying side or addition to a grain bowl with Coriander Chili Hummus Bowl (page 223).

2 tablespoons (30 mL) avocado oil, divided

1 tablespoon (15 mL) ground coffee

1 tablespoon (15 mL) pure maple syrup

¾ teaspoon (3 mL) salt, divided, plus more for seasoning

¾ teaspoon (3 mL) ground cumin, divided

Freshly cracked black pepper

1½ pounds (675 g) carrots, scrubbed, trimmed, and cut in half lengthwise (cut in quarters if larger than 1 inch/2.5 cm in diameter)

1 cup (250 mL) cooked French lentils (firm, not mushy; see Note)

For serving

¼ cup (60 mL) packed fresh curly parsley leaves and tender stems, minced

¼ cup (60 mL) packed fresh mint leaves, minced

Zest of ¼ orange

1. Preheat the oven to 425°F (220°C). Line a baking sheet with parchment paper.

2. In a medium bowl, whisk together 1 tablespoon (15 mL) of the avocado oil, coffee, maple syrup, ½ teaspoon (2 mL) of the salt, ½ teaspoon (2 mL) of the cumin, and some pepper. Add the carrots and toss thoroughly in the mixture to coat. Transfer the mixture to the prepared baking sheet and spread in an even layer.

3. To the same bowl (no need to wipe), add the remaining 1 tablespoon (15 mL) avocado oil, the remaining ¼ teaspoon (1 mL) salt, and the remaining ¼ teaspoon (1 mL) cumin and stir. Add the lentils, mix, and spoon over the carrots on the baking sheet. Roast until the carrots are soft and golden and the lentils are crispy, 35 to 40 minutes, stirring once after 20 minutes.

4. Transfer the roasted carrot and lentil mixture to a serving platter. Sprinkle with the parsley, mint, and orange zest, and season with salt and pepper to taste. Store leftovers in an airtight container in the fridge for up to 3 days. (They are delicious cold as part of a salad or grain bowl.)

Note: Du Puy lentils are also good in this recipe, but they cook fast. If using, add them to the baking sheet at the 20-minute mark.

King Oyster Mushrooms with Wheat Berries and Miso Butter

Serves 2 as a main or 4 as a side

Nut-Free

Vegan

It's incredible how a little extra time, or care, can transform an ingredient into something new. King oyster mushrooms have a firm, meaty flavour that deserves to take centre stage more often. Cross-hatching the mushroom creates little nooks and crannies to soak up a delicious sweet and salty maple miso butter. Be sure to press down on the mushrooms while cooking to ensure direct contact between the mushroom and the hot pan, browning the surface of the mushroom evenly for even more flavour. Served on a bed of chewy wheat berries, this dish makes a nice light meal alongside the Swiss Chard Goma-ae (page 61) for a dose of greens.

1¼ pounds (565 g) king oyster mushrooms

¼ cup (60 mL) vegan butter, at room temperature

1 tablespoon (15 mL) white miso

1 tablespoon (15 mL) pure maple syrup

1 tablespoon (15 mL) soy sauce

1 tablespoon (15 mL) rice vinegar

2 tablespoons (30 mL) avocado or refined coconut oil

1 cup (250 mL) cooked wheat berries

Salt and freshly cracked black pepper

2 green onions, trimmed and thinly sliced on the diagonal

1. Cut the mushrooms in half lengthwise. Using a paring knife, carefully score the flat side of the mushrooms one way and then the other, creating a diamond cross-hatch pattern, cutting about halfway through the mushrooms.

2. In a small bowl, mix together the butter, miso, maple syrup, soy sauce, and rice vinegar.

3. Heat the avocado oil in a large nonstick skillet over medium heat. Work in batches if needed so you do not crowd the pan. Place the mushrooms cut side down in the pan and cook, gently pressing down on the mushrooms with tongs until liquid is released and they turn golden brown, 4 to 6 minutes per side.

4. Reduce the heat to medium-low. Pour the sauce over the mushrooms and stir in the wheat berries. Cook, stirring frequently, until the sauce reduces to a glaze, 2 to 3 minutes. Transfer to a serving dish. Season well with salt and pepper and top with the green onions. Store leftovers in an airtight container in the fridge for up to 2 days. Reheat in a nonstick skillet over medium heat with a splash of water to help restore the sauce.

Brussels Sprouts with Apple and Miso Pecan Butter

Serves 4

Gluten-Free
Vegan

2 tablespoons (30 mL) avocado oil

1¼ pounds (565 g) Brussels sprouts, trimmed and halved

Flaky sea salt

½ crisp apple (such as Ambrosia or Gala), cored, quartered, and thinly sliced using a mandoline

1 tablespoon (15 mL) pure maple syrup

Pinch of red chili flakes

½ batch Miso Pecan Butter (page 299)

Without a doubt, my favourite way to spend a night out (or in!) is sharing a meal with friends. In fact, a lot of my cooking inspiration, whether a flavour combination or an entire dish, comes from those evenings. And this recipe is my at-home take on the fried Brussels sprouts with a red miso–spiked pecan butter I could not get out of my head after enjoying it at Published on Main in Vancouver. It's a deceptively simple recipe with big flavour. I like to make a whole batch of the miso pecan butter to make the equally delicious and simple Soba with Miso Pecan Butter (page 141) the next day.

1. Heat the avocado oil in a large skillet over medium heat. Place the Brussels sprouts cut side down in the pan, cover with a lid, and slightly reduce the heat. Cook until golden brown on the bottom, 6 to 7 minutes. Check after 5 minutes to avoid burning. Flip the sprouts, reduce the heat to medium-low, cover with the lid, and cook until golden brown on the other side, another 4 to 5 minutes. Remove from the heat. Season generously with flaky sea salt. Add the apple, maple syrup, and chili flakes, and toss to combine.

2. Spread the miso pecan butter on the bottom of a serving platter. Pile the Brussels sprouts and apple mixture over the miso pecan butter and serve. Store leftovers in an airtight container in the fridge for up to 2 days. Reheat in a medium skillet over medium heat with a little water. The sauce will thin and coat the Brussels sprouts nicely.

Sumac-Roasted Eggplant with Maple Tahini Drizzle

Every recipe I create for my books reflects a facet of how I like to eat in real life. I cannot write a cookbook without an eggplant recipe (or two!) because I love this vegetable so much. I will happily gobble up all four servings of this eggplant—roasted until its flesh is creamy, sprinkled with citrusy sumac and fresh mint, and drizzled with maple syrup-spiked tahini—with zero complaints.

Serves 4

Gluten-Free

Low-FODMAP Option

Nut-Free

Vegan

Sumac-Roasted Eggplant

4 Chinese eggplants

2 tablespoons (30 mL) avocado oil

1¼ teaspoons (6 mL) ground sumac, plus more for serving

½ teaspoon (2 mL) salt

Freshly cracked black pepper

Maple Tahini Drizzle

2 tablespoons (30 mL) tahini

1 tablespoon (15 mL) pure maple syrup

1 tablespoon (15 mL) water

⅛ teaspoon (0.5 mL) salt

For serving

Flaky sea salt

⅓ cup (75 mL) packed fresh mint leaves, thinly sliced

1. **Roast the eggplant:** Preheat the oven to 400°F (200°C). Line a baking sheet with parchment paper.

2. Cut the eggplants in half lengthwise. Using a paring knife, score the halves diagonally, spaced ½ inch (1 cm) apart. Place the eggplant cut side up on the prepared baking sheet.

3. Brush the eggplant with the avocado oil. Sprinkle with the sumac, salt, and lots of pepper. Turn the eggplant halves over so they are cut side down on the baking sheet. Transfer to the oven and roast until soft and golden brown on the cut side, about 45 minutes.

4. **Meanwhile, make the maple tahini drizzle:** In a small bowl, whisk together the tahini, maple syrup, water, and salt.

5. To serve, pile the eggplant on a serving platter. Spoon the maple tahini drizzle over the eggplant. Sprinkle with a bit more sumac, flaky sea salt, and mint. Store leftovers in an airtight container in the fridge for up to 2 days. (I like to chop and fry the leftover eggplant, then add a bit of water and any leftover maple tahini drizzle until warmed through.)

Swaps + Stuff

1 cup (250 mL) of eggplant is a low-FODMAP serving.

Carrot and Parsnip Fries with Tahini Garlic Aioli

There's something you need to know if we're going to be friends: I take my fries with (vegan) mayo, not ketchup, thank you very much. And as luck would have it, that approach serves us very well even when those fries are tender roasted carrots and parsnips, scented with thyme and drizzled with—or dunked into—a simple, addictive tahini garlic aioli that will have even the parsnip skeptics at your table going back for seconds.

Serves 4
Gluten-Free
Low-FODMAP Option
Nut-Free
Vegan

Carrot and Parsnip Fries

1 pound (450 g) carrots, scrubbed

1 pound (450 g) parsnips, scrubbed and peeled

3 tablespoons (45 mL) avocado or extra-virgin olive oil

1 teaspoon (5 mL) salt

1 teaspoon (5 mL) garlic powder

½ teaspoon (2 mL) dried thyme

Freshly cracked black pepper

2 tablespoons (30 mL) minced fresh curly parsley leaves and tender stems

Tahini Garlic Aioli

½ cup (125 mL) vegan mayonnaise

¼ cup (60 mL) tahini

2 tablespoons (30 mL) freshly squeezed lemon juice

½ teaspoon (2 mL) salt

1 clove garlic, grated on a microplane

2 tablespoons (30 mL) minced fresh curly parsley leaves

1. **Make the carrot and parsnip fries:** Preheat the oven to 425°F (220°C). Line a baking sheet with parchment paper.

2. Cut the carrots and parsnips into uniform sticks so the fries cook evenly, about 4 inches (10 cm) long and ⅓ inch (8 mm) wide.

3. Place the carrot and parsnip sticks in a large bowl. Add the avocado oil, salt, garlic powder, thyme, and pepper to taste, and toss to coat. Evenly spread the sticks on the prepared baking sheet and bake until softened and golden brown, 20 to 25 minutes, turning halfway through. Transfer the fries to a serving dish and sprinkle with the parsley.

4. **Meanwhile, make the tahini garlic aioli:** In a small bowl, whisk together the mayonnaise, tahini, lemon juice, salt, garlic, and parsley until smooth.

5. Serve the fries with the aioli drizzled over top or on the side. Leftover fries and aioli can be stored, in separate airtight containers, in the fridge for up to 3 days.

Swaps + Stuff

For a low-FODMAP version, omit the garlic and garlic powder and swap a garlic-flavoured oil for the avocado oil to make the roasted carrots and parsnip fries.

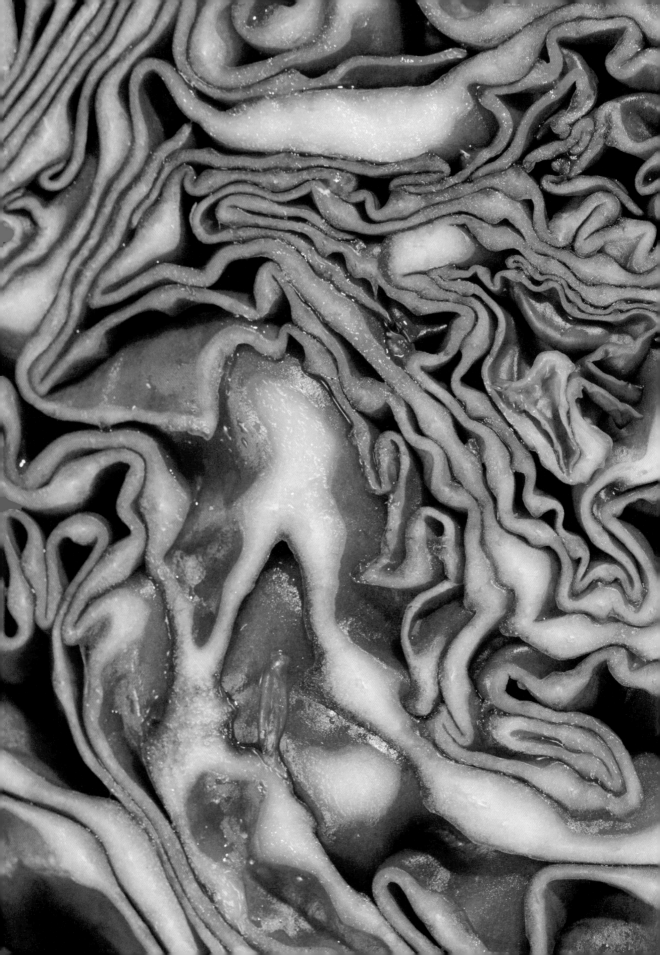

Nutrition Is Dead, Long Live Nutrition

I have devoted more than half of my life to the study and practice of nutrition. I love this stuff. And if you're here, I suspect you do too. That's no small feat. It took us a long time (and tons of science) to get to the point where we recognize that nutrition plays a role in our wellbeing. Even in my own practice, I have encountered plenty of clients whose physicians told them that nutrition won't be of much help. Which obviously is incorrect, but it just goes to show that the nutrition revolution is a very big deal.

For those of us who are living with diabetes or irritable bowel disease (IBS), or even just those of us trying to live a long and healthy life, understanding the transformative power of nutrition is a very good thing, in theory. The way you eat can help you keep your blood sugars balanced, challenging the notion that diabetes is always a progressive disease. Good nutrition can help you feel energized so that you can get the most out of life. Food really does have the power to help you heal.

But when I pick up my phone and see what counts as nutrition information, I cringe. Things like "what I eat in a day" videos that begin with a bikini selfie, as if copying that person's diet will make you look like them. I see people who say that processed food is harmful in one breath and then try to sell a processed protein powder in the next. Nutrition has become a perverse sort of pastime, engaged with on a tiny screen that has well-documented negative effects on our mental health. We read books that claim whole foods are toxic and listen to podcasts that don't have the ability to fact-check their guests. We develop attachments to charismatic, glossy wellness folks, and when they tell us that oat milk is inflammatory, we're inclined to believe them.

This is not the role that nutrition is meant to play: it is meant to be a tool to help us feel our best and help us heal when we don't. We're not meant to think about it 24/7! Our heads fill with ideas—some good, some not so good—that stick with us for life like a bad tattoo. Like how we haven't eaten tofu in a decade because someone told us soy was bad for us when we were in college (it's not). And should our health take a turn, this noise can become a constant source of anxiety.

As many times as I have daydreamed about moving to the country and deleting Instagram, I'm not advocating that we all move off the grid. Actually, access to information can be incredibly empowering, especially for those who don't have access to high-quality care because of their location or resources. Good information gives you the power to make better choices for yourself. But when I think about how much louder the bad information is, sometimes I wonder if we shouldn't just scrap it altogether. In fact, I think most of us might be happier and, ironically, more well if we stopped listening to wellness advice. But since this is unlikely to happen, perhaps setting some clear boundaries is a good idea.

Since wellness practitioners are going to keep doing their thing, it's up to us to (a) disengage from the chaos and (b) know how to spot a fake. It's time we learn to prioritize our actual wellbeing over a strict set of rules that someone else made up about what is healthy. We get to choose what healthy looks like for ourselves. If wellness information makes us feel confused, anxious, or guilty about our food choices, do not pass go—just unfollow. If you choose to engage with wellness information, curate a small selection of positive and supportive practitioners whom you trust to influence your wellness practices.

Sounds simple, yes? I wouldn't be the dietitian I am without acknowledging that getting to this magical place of grounded self-care takes work. And time. It took me decades. The first step is acknowledging that much of what we call wellness is really Diet Culture in disguise. The fearmongering. The gatekeeping. The demanding (and expensive) regimes. This diet-driven mentality challenges our relationship with food and our bodies, as well as robbing us of the joy of eating. So many of the messages we receive from wellness advocates, including actual licensed health professionals, are based on averting some imagined danger, be it inflammation or toxins or whatever. Why? Because internet algorithms favour strong messaging that elicits an emotional response from you. You're more likely to watch a video that starts with "Did you know that oat milk is toxic?" than "Yes, you can eat potato chips and still be healthy."

Critical to the next phase of your wellness re-education—and ensuring that you don't go running back into the algorithmic fray—is reminding yourself that no one ingredient, food, or meal will make or break your health. Pattern over plate, always. You need to let this one sink into your bones because we are still inundated with messaging about cheat days, guilt-free food, and detoxes. The single most effective detox in wellness is hitting the unsubscribe button.

After a lifetime of food rules, welcoming unrestricted eating into your life might feel untethering. A trusted friend, non-diet dietitian, or counsellor can help you through that. There will be a lot of unlearning to do. And it will take time to trust your newly unrestricted food choices. It's about intention, working toward food neutrality, celebrating the abundance of plants and, of course, focusing on flavour. Because feeling good is as much about welcoming joy and pleasure into your life as it is about eating your greens. It's part of the equation, not just an approved indulgence.

Whole Roasted Cauliflower with Green Olive Dressing

Serves 6
Gluten-Free
Nut-Free
Vegan

As far as vegetables go, there are probably none as versatile as cauliflower, and I love the drama of carving into a whole cauliflower at the table. Dredged in an earthy, smoky paprika-spiked rub and topped with a bright and acidic dressing, this is a beautiful dish for a weekend meal with friends alongside Black Olive and Za'atar Focaccia (page 224) and Greek-Style Gigantes Beans in Tomato Sauce (page 195).

Whole Roasted Cauliflower

2 pounds (900 g) head cauliflower, leaves removed and stem ends trimmed

2 tablespoons (30 mL) avocado oil

1 tablespoon (15 mL) smoked paprika

½ teaspoon (2 mL) garlic powder

½ teaspoon (2 mL) ground coriander

½ teaspoon (2 mL) ground cumin

½ teaspoon (2 mL) salt

Green Olive Dressing

½ cup (125 mL) pitted Castelvetrano olives

½ cup (125 mL) lightly packed fresh curly parsley leaves and tender stems

¼ medium shallot, roughly chopped

1 clove garlic

3 tablespoons (45 mL) freshly squeezed lemon juice

2 tablespoons (30 mL) extra-virgin olive or avocado oil

½ teaspoon (2 mL) salt

Freshly cracked black pepper, to taste

Red chili flakes, to taste

1. **Roast the cauliflower:** Preheat the oven to 400°F (200°C). Line a baking sheet with parchment paper.

2. Place the cauliflower on the prepared baking sheet.

3. In a small bowl, whisk together the avocado oil, smoked paprika, garlic powder, coriander, cumin, and salt. Using your hands or a silicone brush, rub the oil mixture all over the exterior of the cauliflower. Transfer to the oven and roast until the cauliflower is fork-tender but not falling apart, 50 to 55 minutes.

4. **Meanwhile, make the green olive dressing:** (It's ideal to make the dressing right after you have popped the cauliflower in the oven, so the flavours have time to meld.) In a small food processor, combine the olives, parsley, shallot, and garlic. Pulse until finely chopped. Scrape the mixture into a small bowl.

5. Whisk the lemon juice, olive oil, salt, pepper, and chili flakes into the olive mixture. The flavour of the shallot will mellow as the dressing sits until ready to use. Taste before serving; if you need to balance out an overly strong shallot, just add a pinch of sugar.

6. Remove the roasted cauliflower from the oven and let rest on the baking sheet for 5 minutes. Serve the cauliflower whole or cut into wedges on a medium platter, drizzled with the green olive dressing. Store leftovers in an airtight container in the fridge for up to 3 days.

Roasted Beets with **Tahini Yogurt, Za'atar,** and **Hazelnuts**

Serves 4
Gluten-Free
Nut-Free Option
Vegan

If you've got friends coming over, make this! It offers big, balanced flavour—sweet, earthy, tart, and aromatic—and requires very little hands-on time. Roasting the beets really brings out the best in this incredibly nourishing veg. I use a locally made coconut yogurt that's thick like Greek yogurt; if you don't have access to that, start by using ⅓ cup (75 mL) of yogurt and add more as necessary so you don't end up with an overly runny sauce.

Roasted Beets

1½ pounds (675 g) red beets (about 3 large beets)

2 tablespoons (30 mL) avocado oil

½ teaspoon (2 mL) salt, plus more for seasoning

Freshly cracked black pepper

Tahini Yogurt

¾ cup (175 mL) unsweetened thick coconut yogurt (I use Yoggu!)

¼ cup (60 mL) tahini

3 tablespoons (45 mL) freshly squeezed lemon juice

1 small clove garlic, grated on a microplane

½ teaspoon (2 mL) salt, plus more for seasoning

Freshly cracked black pepper

Pure maple syrup (optional)

For serving

1 tablespoon (15 mL) Simple Za'atar (page 292) or store-bought

¼ cup (60 mL) raw hazelnuts, chopped

1. **Roast the beets:** Preheat the oven to 400° F (200°C). Line a baking sheet with parchment paper.

2. Peel and cut the beets in half. Cut each half into quarters, about 1 inch (2.5 cm) thick. Place the beet wedges on the prepared baking sheet. Toss the beets with the avocado oil, salt, and pepper to taste. The beets should be evenly coated. Roast until fork-tender, 38 to 42 minutes.

3. **Meanwhile, make the tahini yogurt:** In a small bowl, combine the coconut yogurt, tahini, lemon juice, garlic, salt, and pepper to taste. Using a whisk or immersion blender, blend until smooth. Taste, and if you want the yogurt to be sweeter, add the maple syrup, 1 teaspoon (5 mL) at a time, until the flavour is to your taste.

4. To serve, swirl the tahini yogurt across the bottom of a serving dish. Top with the roasted beets, za'atar, hazelnuts, and a pinch each of salt and pepper. Store leftovers in an airtight container in the fridge for up to 3 days.

Swaps + Stuff
For a nut-free version, swap sunflower seeds for the hazelnuts.

Simple and Satisfying Ginger Cabbage

Serves 6

Gluten-Free

Nut-Free

Vegan

What to do with that half a cabbage in the fridge? You could make a slaw, but if you want something warm, make this nourishing, cozy dish. Without a lot of effort, you'll coax even more flavour out of this affordable and nutritious veg. Inspired by Indian sabzi-style cabbage, this is delicious as a side, stuffed into a wrap, or layered into a grain bowl or noodle dish. Coriander and cumin offer a grounding earthy note to the subtle sweetness of the cabbage and onions.

2 tablespoons (30 mL) extra-virgin olive or avocado oil

1 medium yellow onion, thinly sliced into half-moons

1 (1-inch/2.5 cm) piece fresh ginger, peeled and chopped

¾ teaspoon (3 mL) ground coriander

¼ teaspoon (1 mL) ground cumin

1½ pounds (675 g) red or green cabbage, cored and thinly sliced

¾ teaspoon (3 mL) salt

Freshly cracked black pepper

Minced fresh curly parsley leaves and tender stems, for serving (optional)

1. Heat the olive oil in a large skillet over medium heat. Add the onions and ginger and cook, stirring occasionally, until the onions are soft and translucent, 5 to 7 minutes.

2. Stir in the coriander and cumin. Add the cabbage and cook, stirring frequently, until the cabbage is tender-crisp, 5 to 7 minutes. Season with the salt and pepper, taste, and adjust seasoning if needed. Sprinkle with the parsley, if using. Store leftovers in an airtight container in the fridge for up to 2 days.

Charred Broccolini with Romesco-Style Sauce

Serves 4

Gluten-Free

Vegan

Of all the sauces, romesco is one of the greats; hailing from the Catalonia region in Spain, there are as many variations of this beloved condiment as there are cooks. My version leans into simplicity and fresh acidity, substituting jarred roasted red peppers for the traditional roasted tomatoes and dried ñora peppers. If you don't have broccolini, you can substitute thin spears of broccoli. If there are any leftovers, try piling them in a sandwich with some Herbed Cashew Cheese (page 297).

Romesco-Style Sauce

½ cup (125 mL) blanched or slivered almonds

1½ cups (375 mL) jarred roasted red peppers, patted dry

1 tablespoon (15 mL) tomato paste

1 teaspoon (5 mL) sweet paprika

2 cloves garlic

¾ teaspoon (3 mL) salt

2 tablespoons (30 mL) extra-virgin olive oil

2 tablespoons (30 mL) sherry vinegar or red wine vinegar

Broccolini

1 pound (450 g) broccolini, ends trimmed

1 tablespoon (15 mL) extra-virgin olive oil

Salt and freshly cracked black pepper

Lemon wedge

1. **Make the romesco-style sauce:** In a small food processor, pulse the almonds until finely chopped. Add the roasted red peppers, tomato paste, sweet paprika, garlic, and salt. Blend until a thick paste forms. With the processor running, drizzle in the olive oil and sherry vinegar and blend until smooth. Set aside until ready to use or store in an airtight container in the fridge for up to 5 days.

2. **Grill the broccolini:** Preheat a grill to medium (400° to 450°F/200° to 230°C).

3. In a shallow dish, toss the broccolini with the olive oil, and salt and pepper to taste. Grill the broccolini until lightly charred on all sides, 3 to 5 minutes per side. Smaller stalks will be done sooner, so check often.

4. To serve, spread half the sauce in a shallow serving bowl or platter. Pile the broccolini on the sauce and squeeze a bit of lemon juice over top. Serve with the remaining sauce on the side.

Braised Fennel and Lentils

Serves 4 as a light meal

Gluten-Free Option
Nut-Free
Vegan

There are no limits to the different flavours and textures you can create when you're ready to get creative with vegetables in the kitchen. My starting point for this recipe was, "What if we treat fennel like meat?" Searing fennel caramelizes it and softens the overt licorice notes, which then pairs perfectly with the deeply savoury and almost meaty flavour of the lentils. It's a lovely vegetable side dish for a weekend or special occasion meal or a simple yet hearty meal on its own when served with a whole grain.

2 tablespoons (30 mL) extra-virgin olive or avocado oil

2 pounds (900 g) fennel bulbs (2 to 3 medium bulbs), trimmed, fronds reserved, bulbs quartered lengthwise

Freshly cracked black pepper

3 cloves garlic, chopped

1 teaspoon (5 mL) coriander seeds

½ teaspoon (2 mL) fennel seeds

3 cups (750 mL) water

2 teaspoons (10 mL) chicken-flavoured vegetarian stock concentrate or gluten-free vegetable stock

1 bay leaf

1 cup (250 mL) dried French lentils

¼ teaspoon (1 mL) salt, plus more for seasoning

Zest of ½ orange

Flaky sea salt

1. Heat a large heavy-bottomed pot or Dutch oven over medium-high heat. Add the olive oil and fennel wedges and cook until browned, 3 to 4 minutes per side. Work in batches if needed so you do not crowd the pan. Reduce the heat to medium if the oil starts smoking. Once the fennel is browned, transfer to a plate and season to taste with salt and pepper.

2. Place the same pot (no need to wipe) over medium heat. Add the garlic, coriander seeds, and fennel seeds and cook, stirring constantly, for 1 minute. Add the water, stock concentrate, bay leaf, lentils, and salt. Bring to a full boil over high heat for 2 minutes, then reduce the heat to medium-low. Return the fennel to the pot, cover with the lid slightly ajar, and simmer until the lentils are soft, 18 to 22 minutes. Remove from the heat. Taste and adjust the seasoning if needed. Discard the bay leaf.

3. To serve, scoop the lentils into a shallow serving bowl. Top with the fennel wedges and sprinkle with the orange zest and reserved fennel fronds. Ladle a bit of cooking liquid over top. Finish with flaky sea salt and more pepper. Store leftovers in an airtight container in the fridge for up to 2 days. (When reheating, I like to turn this into more of a soup by chopping the fennel and adding extra water.)

Swaps + Stuff

For a gluten-free version, use gluten-free stock concentrate or gluten-free vegetable stock.

Smashed Potatoes with Bravas-Style Paprika Gravy

This is my cheeky take on the classic Spanish dish patatas bravas, chunks of fried potatoes served with aioli and paprika-spiked gravy. Instead of frying the potatoes, they are smashed and baked so that the oil can crisp up the skin, giving you plenty of texture. You usually see recipes for bravas sauce made with tomatoes or tomato paste, but in researching this recipe, I discovered that the sauce pre-dates the arrival of tomatoes in Europe. So I decided to try my hand at developing a true paprika gravy that feels like magic as you watch it instantly thicken in the pot.

Serves 6 as a side

Gluten-Free
Low-FODMAP Option
Nut-Free
Vegan

Smashed Potatoes

2 pounds (900 g) small or medium red-skinned potatoes, scrubbed

1 tablespoon (15 mL) + ½ teaspoon (2 mL) salt, divided

¼ cup (60 mL) avocado or extra-virgin olive oil

1 teaspoon (5 mL) chopped fresh rosemary leaves (or ½ teaspoon/2 mL dried rosemary)

Freshly cracked black pepper

Bravas-Style Paprika Gravy

¼ cup (60 mL) extra-virgin olive oil

1 tablespoon (15 mL) cornstarch

1 tablespoon (15 mL) sweet paprika

1 teaspoon (5 mL) smoked paprika

½ teaspoon (2 mL) garlic powder

1 cup (250 mL) low-sodium vegetable broth

2 teaspoons (10 mL) sherry vinegar

½ teaspoon (2 mL) salt

1. **Make the smashed potatoes:** Preheat the oven to 425°F (220°C). Line a baking sheet with parchment paper.

2. Bring a large pot of water to a boil over high heat. Add the potatoes and 1 tablespoon (15 mL) of the salt and cook, uncovered, until fork-tender, 10 to 16 minutes (depending on the size of the potatoes). Drain and let cool for 5 minutes in a colander.

3. Spread the boiled potatoes on the prepared baking sheet. Using the bottom of a measuring cup, gently smash each potato until about ½ inch (1 cm) thick. Drizzle with the avocado oil. Sprinkle the rosemary, the remaining ½ teaspoon (2 mL) salt, and lots of pepper over the potatoes. Transfer to the oven and roast until the potatoes are golden brown and crispy around the edges, 25 to 35 minutes.

4. **Meanwhile, make the bravas-style paprika gravy:** In a small saucepan over medium heat, whisk together the olive oil, cornstarch, sweet paprika, smoked paprika, and garlic powder until the mixture is bubbling. Once bubbling, slowly add the vegetable broth, 1 to 2 tablespoons (15 to 30 mL) at a time, whisking constantly as it thickens. You want to maintain the bubbling to ensure that the mixture thickens instantly. If you add too much liquid at once, it may break the gravy (see Note). Once all the broth is added, let the mixture bubble for 1 minute.

Remove from the heat and whisk in the sherry vinegar and salt. The gravy will continue to thicken as it cools.

5. To serve, arrange the roasted potatoes on a serving platter and drizzle with half the bravas-style paprika gravy. Serve the remaining gravy on the side. Store leftover potatoes and gravy, in separate airtight containers, in the fridge for up to 3 days.

Note: If you accidently add the broth too fast and the mixture doesn't thicken, you can save it! Place another 1 tablespoon (15 mL) of cornstarch and 2 to 3 tablespoons (30 to 45 mL) of gravy in a small bowl and mix to combine. Then add it back to the gravy over medium heat, stir, and let the gravy bubble until thick, about 10 minutes.

Swaps + Stuff

For a low-FODMAP version, omit the garlic powder from the gravy and swap garlic-flavoured oil for the olive oil. Use low-FODMAP vegetable broth.

3 Salads You'll Crave

Chickpea Greek Salad with Creamy Balsamic Dressing

A Greek salad is one of the first meals I learned how to make growing up and is still one of my favourite comfort foods. It inspired this hearty and satisfying chickpea salad, with a punchy, creamy balsamic dressing that is sure to be the hit of your next picnic or potluck. It also makes a great meal prep lunch for the week ahead, as it keeps well. Take the time to dice your veggies so they're about the same size as the chickpeas. It seems like a small thing, but that change in texture really improves the salad.

Serves 6

Gluten-Free

Nut-Free

Vegan

Creamy Balsamic Dressing

¼ cup (60 mL) extra-virgin olive oil

¼ cup (60 mL) balsamic vinegar

4 teaspoons (20 mL) Dijon mustard

2 teaspoons (10 mL) cane sugar

1 teaspoon (5 mL) dried oregano

¾ teaspoon (3 mL) salt

Chickpea Greek Salad

3 cans (14 ounces/398 mL each) chickpeas, rinsed and drained (or 4½ cups/1.1 L cooked chickpeas)

1 cup (250 mL) diced English cucumber

1 cup (250 mL) cherry tomatoes, halved

1 sweet red pepper, diced

1 cup (250 mL) packed fresh curly parsley leaves and tender stems, chopped

½ cup (125 mL) crumbled vegan feta cheese

⅓ cup (75 mL) pitted kalamata olives, halved

¼ cup (60 mL) packed fresh dill, chopped

½ medium shallot, finely chopped

1. **Make the creamy balsamic dressing:** In a 1-cup (250 mL) mason jar, combine the olive oil, balsamic vinegar, mustard, sugar, oregano, and salt. Screw the lid on tightly and shake.

2. **Make the chickpea Greek salad:** In a large serving bowl, combine the chickpeas, cucumber, tomatoes, sweet pepper, parsley, feta, olives, dill, and shallot. Drizzle the creamy balsamic dressing over the salad and toss to coat. Store the dressed salad in an airtight container in the fridge for up to 4 days.

Tomato and Date Salad with Tahini Lemon Dressing

My love of tahini in all its savoury, earthy glory is no secret. But I didn't realize what a perfect match it was for tomatoes until I sat down a few years ago to a tomato salad with a lemon tahini dressing so addictive that I was trying to discreetly slurp up the extras with my spoon! This lovely salad, studded with dates and mint is light, refreshing, and right at home in a snack spread alongside my Coriander Chili Hummus Bowl (page 223) and Roasted Eggplant Dip with Sundried Tomato and Walnuts (page 229).

Serves 6 as a side

Gluten-Free

Nut-Free

Vegan

Lemon Tahini Dressing

¼ cup (60 mL) freshly squeezed lemon juice

¼ cup (60 mL) extra-virgin olive oil

2 tablespoons (30 mL) tahini

1 tablespoon (15 mL) pure maple syrup

¾ teaspoon (3 mL) salt

½ clove garlic, crushed or grated on a microplane

Freshly cracked black pepper

Tomato and Date Salad

2 pints (4 cups/1 L) cherry tomatoes, halved

¼ teaspoon (1 mL) salt (optional; see step 2)

⅓ cup (75 mL) lightly packed fresh mint leaves, sliced into thin ribbons

¼ cup (60 mL) pitted Medjool dates, thinly sliced

1. **Make the lemon tahini dressing:** In a small blender or using a wide-mouth blending cup with a handheld immersion blender, combine the lemon juice, olive oil, tahini, maple syrup, salt, garlic, and plenty of pepper. Blend until smooth. The dressing can be stored in an airtight container in the fridge for up to 4 days.

2. **Make the tomato and date salad:** Toss the tomatoes with the salt in a fine-mesh sieve. Place the sieve over a medium bowl and let sit for 15 minutes to drain. (The salt draws out water, helping to intensify the fruits' natural flavours. This will help make supermarket tomatoes even more flavourful. You can skip this step if you have summer-ripe tomatoes.)

3. In a medium salad bowl, toss together the tomatoes, mint, and dates. Divide the salad between plates and drizzle with the lemon tahini dressing. The dressed salad can be stored in an airtight container in the fridge for up to 1 day.

Lentil, Orange, and **Radicchio Salad** with **Mint**

Serves 6 as a side

Gluten-Free

Nut-Free Option

Vegan

Get on board with bitter. In a world dominated by sweet and salty, bitter vegetables like radicchio demand that our taste buds wake up and take notice. This light yet filling salad of protein and fibre-rich lentils reveals layer upon layer of flavour, with sweet and juicy oranges, earthy walnuts, cumin, and plenty of invigorating mint. With the leaves stored separately, it also keeps well for a quick lunch with some whole-grain sourdough when time is tight.

Salad

1¼ cups (300 mL) dried French lentils (about 3 cups/750 mL cooked)

2 medium navel oranges, peeled, pith removed, and cut into ½-inch (1 cm) pieces

½ small head radicchio, finely shredded

½ cup (125 mL) lightly packed fresh mint leaves, thinly sliced

¼ cup (60 mL) raw walnut pieces or chopped walnuts

Dressing

3 tablespoons (45 mL) extra-virgin olive oil

2 tablespoons (30 mL) white wine vinegar or apple cider vinegar

4 teaspoons (20 mL) pure maple syrup

1 clove garlic, crushed or grated on a microplane

½ teaspoon (2 mL) ground cumin

1¼ teaspoons (6 mL) salt

Freshly cracked black pepper

1. **Cook the lentils:** In a medium pot, combine the lentils and 6 cups (1.5 L) of water. Bring to a boil over high heat, then reduce the heat to medium and cook, uncovered, until the lentils are tender but firm, 12 to 16 minutes. Drain in a fine-mesh sieve and rinse under cool running water. Drain again and set aside.

2. **Meanwhile, make the dressing:** In a 1-cup (250 mL) mason jar, combine the olive oil, white wine vinegar, maple syrup, garlic, cumin, salt, and pepper to taste. Screw the lid on tightly and shake.

3. **Assemble the salad:** In a medium salad bowl, combine the lentils, orange pieces, radicchio, mint, and walnuts. Drizzle the dressing over top, toss to combine, and let sit for 10 minutes before serving to allow the flavours to meld. Taste and adjust the salt or maple syrup if needed. Store leftovers the salad in an airtight container in the fridge for up to 2 days. (If you want to store the salad longer, keep the walnuts, mint, and radicchio separate so they retain their texture. Combine all the ingredients when ready to serve.)

Swaps + Stuff

For a nut-free version, swap sunflower seeds for the walnuts.

Corn and Coconut Salad with Cumin Lime Dressing

This is one of those simple recipes that is so much greater than the sum of its parts: salted peanuts, coconut, and corn are such a delicious combination with a juicy hit of cumin lime dressing to liven up any plant party. It's also a great way to use up leftover corn, whether boiled, sautéed, or slightly charred on the grill to add even more flavour to this easy, breezy salad.

Serves 4 as a side

Gluten-Free

Nut-Free Option

Vegan

Corn and Coconut Salad

1 pint (2 cups/500 mL) cherry tomatoes, halved

2 cups (500 mL) fresh or frozen corn kernels, cooked and cooled (from 2 large ears of corn; see Note)

½ cup (125 mL) lightly packed fresh cilantro leaves and tender stems, finely chopped

1 tablespoon (15 mL) minced shallot

½ cup (125 mL) unsweetened large flake coconut (or ¼ cup/60 mL unsweetened shredded coconut)

¼ cup (60 mL) chopped salted peanuts or corn nuts

Cumin Lime Dressing

1 tablespoon (15 mL) avocado oil

2 tablespoons (30 mL) freshly squeezed lime juice

½ clove garlic, grated on a microplane

½ teaspoon (2 mL) salt

¼ teaspoon (1 mL) cane sugar

Pinch of ground cumin

½ jalapeño pepper, seeded and diced (optional)

1. **Make the corn and coconut salad:** In a medium bowl, toss together the tomatoes, corn kernels, cilantro, and shallot.

2. **Make the cumin lime dressing:** In a 1-cup (250 mL) mason jar, combine the avocado oil, lime juice, garlic, salt, sugar, cumin, and jalapeño, if using. Screw the lid on tightly and shake.

3. **Assemble the salad:** Drizzle the dressing over the salad and stir to combine. Sprinkle the coconut and peanuts over the salad. Store the salad, without the coconut and peanuts, in an airtight container in the fridge for up to 3 days. (If you are expecting leftovers, it's nice to keep the peanuts and coconut separate to preserve their crunch. Toss into the salad just before serving.)

Note: If you don't have leftover cooked corn kernels on hand, place the kernels in a small saucepan with 2 tablespoons (30 mL) water and cook over medium heat for 1 to 2 minutes to cook off the starch and enhance sweetness. Drain and use.

Swaps + Stuff

For a nut-free version, use corn nuts instead of peanuts.

Grilled Kale Salad with Spelt and Dried Cherries

Serves 4

Gluten-Free Option

Nut-Free Option

Vegan

If there is one wellness cliché I will proudly admit to embodying, it's my deep and undying love for a good kale salad. As far as greens go, kale's personality skews dark and brooding—lettuce pales in comparison—with a satisfying chew and endless possibilities for transformation. Case in point: it's also very good on the grill. The inspiration for this salad came from my friend Carrie Walder, who shared a genius idea of using grilled kale in a salad, which essentially turns the ends into kale chips to lighten up the texture while doubling down on flavour.

- 2 tablespoons (30 mL) avocado oil, divided, plus more for brushing the lemon
- 1 pound (450 g) curly kale, destemmed
- 1 lemon, halved
- Freshly cracked black pepper
- 1 tablespoon (15 mL) nutritional yeast
- 2 teaspoons (10 mL) pure maple syrup
- 1 small garlic clove, grated on a microplane
- ½ teaspoon (2 mL) salt, plus more for seasoning
- 1 cup (250 mL) cooked spelt (about ⅓ cup/75 mL dried spelt)
- ¼ cup (60 mL) dried cherries or cranberries
- ¼ cup (60 mL) chopped raw almonds or sunflower seeds

1. Preheat a grill to medium heat (400° to 450°F/200° to 230°C).

2. Pour 1 tablespoon (15 mL) of the avocado oil into a small bowl. Brush the kale leaves very lightly with the oil, just enough to avoid the edges sticking to the grill, otherwise the kale will be oily. Place the kale on a baking sheet so you can easily transfer them to the grill. Brush the lemon halves with avocado oil and place them on the baking sheet.

3. Place the largest kale leaves on the grill first since they will take a bit longer to cook, and work in batches if necessary. Place the lemon halves cut side down at the back of the grill, where it is usually hottest. Grill the kale until the edges are slightly charred and they look like kale chips, 1 to 3 minutes per side. Keep an eye on the kale so it doesn't burn. Remove the kale from the grill and return it to the baking sheet. The lemon is done once grill marks are visible, which may take a couple of minutes more than the kale. Season the kale with a bit of salt and pepper.

4. In a medium serving bowl, whisk together the remaining 1 tablespoon (15 mL) avocado oil, nutritional yeast, maple syrup, garlic, salt, and pepper to taste. Juice half a grilled lemon into the dressing (scoop out any seeds) and whisk. If it's a juicy lemon, that may be all you need. Taste and, if too sweet, juice the remaining grilled lemon half and add, a little at a time, to the dressing until you like the balance of acidity.

5. Add the grilled kale, spelt, dried cherries, and almonds to the bowl with the dressing. Taste and adjust the salt if needed. Toss well to coat. Store leftovers in an airtight container in the fridge for up to 2 days.

Swaps + Stuff

For a gluten-free version, swap cooked quinoa or rice for the spelt.

For a nut-free version, use sunflower seeds instead of almonds.

Brined Rice Salad with Pomegranate and Pistachio

Serves 4 to 6
Gluten-Free
Low-FODMAP Option
Vegan

This richly hued and flavourful rice salad is inspired by the colours and flavours of Persian cuisine, which is resplendent with dried fruit, nuts, fresh herbs, and spices. Although this salad relies on many traditional ingredients, such as basmati rice, lemony sumac, and tangy pomegranate molasses, it is distinctly non-traditional. The rice is coloured with turmeric, as opposed to saffron. Adding dill pickle brine to the cooking liquid uses up a commonly discarded foodstuff and subtly enhances the dill flavour without overpowering the rice.

Brined Rice Salad

1 cup (250 mL) white or brown basmati rice

1 cup (250 mL) dill pickle brine

1 cup (250 mL) water

½ teaspoon (2 mL) ground turmeric

1½ cups (375 mL) thinly sliced Persian cucumber

1 cup (250 mL) lightly packed fresh flat-leaf parsley leaves and tender stems, chopped

½ cup (125 mL) lightly packed fresh dill, chopped

½ cup (125 mL) pomegranate arils

½ cup (125 mL) salted pistachios

Pomegranate Sumac Dressing

¼ cup (60 mL) extra-virgin olive oil

2 tablespoons (30 mL) freshly squeezed lime juice

1 tablespoon (15 mL) pomegranate molasses

1½ teaspoons (7 mL) ground sumac

1 teaspoon (5 mL) cane sugar

½ teaspoon (2 mL) salt

Freshly cracked black pepper

1. **Cook the rice:** In a small pot, combine the rice, dill pickle brine, water, and turmeric. Bring to a boil over high heat, then reduce the heat to medium-low, cover with the lid slightly ajar, and simmer until the rice is tender and the liquid is absorbed, 30 minutes. Remove from the heat, fluff the rice with a fork, cover with the lid, and let sit for 10 minutes. Spread the rice on a parchment-lined baking sheet to help it cool to room temperature.

2. **Meanwhile, make the pomegranate sumac dressing:** In a small bowl, whisk together the olive oil, lime juice, pomegranate molasses, sumac, sugar, salt, and pepper to taste. Set aside.

3. **Assemble the salad:** In a large salad bowl, toss together the cooled rice, cucumbers, parsley, dill, pomegranate arils, and pistachios. Drizzle half the dressing over top and toss. Store the salad and the remaining dressing separately in airtight containers in the fridge for up to 3 days. (When stored, the salad tends to soak up the dressing and the flavour dulls a bit. Brighten up leftovers with the remaining dressing.)

Swaps + Stuff

For a low-FODMAP version, use ¼ cup (60 mL) of pomegranate arils and swap another 1 tablespoon (15 mL) of lime juice for the 1 tablespoon (15 mL) pomegranate molasses.

Kohlrabi Peanut Slaw

Serves 4 as a side

Gluten-Free Option

Low-FODMAP Option

Nut-Free Option

Vegan

If you've ever looked at a knobby bulb of kohlrabi at the farmers' market and wondered, "What the heck do I do with that?", this recipe is for you. Kohlrabi has a mild flavour, somewhat similar to broccoli stalks. When grated, kohlrabi trades its signature crunch for a satisfying tenderness in this simple slaw inspired by Thai green papaya salad. Ready in less than twenty minutes, with a fresh and fiery dressing and crunchy salted peanuts, it will leave you excited to explore this wonderful vegetable.

1 pound (450 g) kohlrabi, peeled and grated

1 teaspoon (5 mL) salt

3 tablespoons (45 mL) freshly squeezed lime juice

1½ teaspoons (7 mL) cane sugar

½ teaspoon (2 mL) soy sauce or gluten-free tamari

¼ to ½ fresh Thai red chili, thinly sliced

⅓ cup (75 mL) salted peanuts, chopped

¼ cup (60 mL) lightly packed fresh mint leaves

1. Place the grated kohlrabi in a fine-mesh sieve. Toss with the salt and place the sieve over a medium bowl for 10 minutes to draw the water out of the kohlrabi.

2. Meanwhile, in a medium bowl, whisk together the lime juice, sugar, soy sauce, and Thai chili.

3. Squeeze excess liquid from the kohlrabi and place the kohlrabi in the bowl with the dressing, then toss to evenly coat. Let sit for 5 minutes to let the flavours meld. Sprinkle the peanuts and mint over the slaw. Store leftovers in an airtight container in the fridge for up to 2 days.

Swaps + Stuff

For a nut-free version, swap salted corn nuts for the peanuts.

For a gluten-free version, use gluten-free tamari.

½ cup (125 mL) kohlrabi is a low-FODMAP serving.

Warm Brassica Salad with Maple Dijon Dressing

Serves 6 as a side

Gluten-Free

Nut-Free Option

Vegan

Cruciferous vegetables like broccoli and arugula, also known as brassicas, are incredibly nutrient-dense plants that are worthy of a regular spot in your meal rotation, but not everyone is as enamoured with them as I am. I'm hoping that this salad will change that. Roasting brings out a sweeter, toasty side of broccoli that is made even more enjoyable with a maple Dijon dressing and sweet Medjool dates. I love eating a big bowl of this salad with boiled or roasted lentils as a main.

Warm Brassica Salad

1½ pounds (675 g) broccoli crowns, cut into small florets

2 tablespoons (30 mL) avocado oil

½ teaspoon (2 mL) salt, plus more for seasoning

Freshly cracked black pepper

5 medium unpeeled cloves garlic

¼ cup (60 mL) pitted Medjool dates, thinly sliced

¼ cup (60 mL) chopped raw walnuts, walnut pieces, or raw pumpkin seeds

2 cups (500 mL) packed baby arugula

Maple Dijon Dressing

3 tablespoons (45 mL) freshly squeezed lemon juice

2 tablespoons (30 mL) Dijon mustard

1 tablespoon (15 mL) pure maple syrup

1 tablespoon (15 mL) avocado oil

½ teaspoon (2 mL) salt

Large pinch of red chili flakes

1. **Roast the broccoli and garlic:** Preheat the oven to 425°F (220°C). Line a baking sheet with parchment paper.

2. Place the broccoli on the prepared baking sheet. Drizzle with the avocado oil, season with the salt and pepper, and toss to coat. Nestle in the garlic cloves and roast until the broccoli is well browned, 25 to 30 minutes. Check the garlic cloves after 20 minutes so they don't brown, removing them if necessary. Let the broccoli cool on the baking sheet for 5 minutes.

3. **Meanwhile, make the maple Dijon dressing:** In a large salad bowl, whisk together the lemon juice, mustard, maple syrup, avocado oil, salt, and chili flakes. Squeeze the garlic cloves to pop out the roasted garlic. Whisk the roasted garlic into the dressing.

4. **Assemble the salad:** Add the cooled broccoli, dates, and walnuts to the bowl with the dressing and toss to evenly coat. Add the arugula and toss again. Taste, and adjust the salt if needed. Serve warm or at room temperature. Store leftovers in an airtight container in the fridge for up to 2 days.

Swaps + Stuff

For a nut-free version, use pumpkin seeds instead of walnuts.

Sunshine Panzanella

Serves 4 as a side

Gluten-Free Option

Nut-Free

Vegan

Panzanella is a showstopper of a salad with humble origins. Predating the arrival of tomatoes in Italy, it began simply as a way of soaking stale bread to revive it, perhaps with the addition of some onion. I've swapped the usual tomatoes for another summer staple—peaches— alongside sunny golden beets and cool, refreshing fennel. Believe me when I say that this is as close to a perfect summer salad as it gets.

Salad

1 large golden beet, peeled, halved, and cut into ½-inch (1 cm) wedges

2 tablespoons (30 mL) extra-virgin olive oil, divided

Salt and freshly cracked black pepper

4 cups (1 L) day-old torn or cubed crusty whole-grain sourdough bread

2 ripe medium peaches, pitted and thinly sliced

1 cup (250 mL) thinly sliced fennel (about ½ small bulb)

½ cup (125 mL) thinly sliced red onion

½ cup (125 mL) lightly packed fresh basil leaves, thinly sliced

1 sprig fresh thyme, leaves only

Dressing

¼ cup (60 mL) extra-virgin olive oil

2 tablespoons (30 mL) balsamic vinegar

2 tablespoons (30 mL) freshly squeezed lemon juice

2 cloves garlic, crushed or grated on a microplane

1 teaspoon (5 mL) Dijon mustard

1 teaspoon (5 mL) salt

Freshly cracked black pepper

1. **Roast the beets:** Preheat the oven to 400°F (200°C). Line a baking sheet with parchment paper.

2. Place the beets on one third of the prepared baking sheet. Toss the beets with 1 tablespoon (15 mL) of the olive oil, a pinch of salt, and some pepper. Roast for 15 minutes. Remove from the oven.

3. **Prep and toast the bread:** In a medium bowl, toss the bread with the remaining 1 tablespoon (15 mL) olive oil, a pinch of salt, and some pepper. Transfer the coated bread to the baking sheet alongside the beets and return to the oven. Roast until the beets are fork-tender but not too soft and the bread is toasted and crisp around the edges, 10 to 12 minutes. Remove from the oven.

4. **Meanwhile, make the dressing:** In a 1-cup (250 mL) mason jar, combine the olive oil, balsamic vinegar, lemon juice, garlic, mustard, salt, and pepper to taste. Screw the lid on tightly and shake.

5. **Assemble the salad:** In a large serving bowl or on a platter, combine the toasted bread, beets, peaches, fennel, red onion, basil, and thyme. Pour the dressing over top, toss to coat, and let sit for 10 minutes before serving so the bread can soak up the dressing. Store in an airtight container in the fridge for up to 2 days.

Swaps + Stuff

For a gluten-free version, swap your favourite gluten-free bakery loaf for the sourdough bread.

Broccoli Salad with **Tahini Ranch**

Serves 6 as a side

Gluten-Free

Nut-Free

Vegan

This is not your mama's broccoli salad. It's tahini! It's ranch! It's a punchy take on a classic with the flavour dialled up to one hundred. Take the time to cut the broccoli into small florets so there are more nooks and crannies for this delicious dressing to cling to every bite. This salad is at home with hot dogs (veggie, of course!) at a barbecue or on a snack table with Carrot and Za'atar Pancakes (page 231) and Spicy Tofu Nuggets (page 240). If you like your ranch a bit more subdued, omit the apple cider vinegar and add a bit more maple syrup.

Tahini Ranch

⅓ cup (75 mL) tahini

⅓ cup (75 mL) freshly squeezed lemon juice

2 tablespoons (30 mL) extra-virgin olive oil or avocado oil

2 tablespoons (30 mL) water

1 tablespoon (15 mL) apple cider vinegar (optional; omit if you like a less tangy ranch)

1½ teaspoons (7 mL) garlic powder

1 teaspoon (5 mL) onion powder

1 teaspoon (5 mL) salt

1 teaspoon (5 mL) pure maple syrup, plus more as needed

¼ cup (60 mL) lightly packed fresh dill, minced

2 tablespoons (30 mL) finely chopped fresh chives

Freshly cracked black pepper

Broccoli Salad

1 pound (450 g) broccoli crowns, cut into small florets

¼ cup (60 mL) raw sunflower seeds or slivered almonds

¼ cup (60 mL) pitted Medjool dates, thinly sliced

1. **Make the tahini ranch:** In a large salad bowl, whisk together the tahini, lemon juice, olive oil, water, apple cider vinegar (if using), garlic powder, onion powder, salt, and maple syrup. Stir in the dill, chives, and some pepper. Taste and adjust with a bit more maple syrup if too sour.

2. **Assemble the broccoli salad:** Add the broccoli, sunflower seeds, and dates to the bowl with the dressing and toss well to ensure that the broccoli is evenly coated. This salad is great made 30 minutes ahead of serving to allow the flavours to meld. Store leftovers in an airtight container in the fridge for up to 3 days.

Herby Potato Salad with Grainy Mustard Vinaigrette

Serves 6 as a side

Gluten-Free

Low-FODMAP

Nut-Free

Vegan

If I were to suggest a food to eat daily, it would be greens. And herbs are easily the most unsung member of the green and leafy family. Their deep hues and vibrant flavours are due to an abundance of phytochemicals with antioxidant and anti-inflammatory properties that we could all use a little more of in this modern world. This potato salad, studded with herbs and a tangy, mustardy dressing is delicious alongside Cumin Lime Black Bean Burgers (page 163) or West Coast Hippie Sandwiches (page 171).

Herby Potato Salad

2 pounds (900 g) baby potatoes, halved or quartered

1 can (14 ounces/398 mL) lentils, rinsed and drained well

1 cup (250 mL) lightly packed fresh curly parsley leaves and tender stems, chopped

½ cup (125 mL) lightly packed fresh basil leaves, thinly sliced

¼ cup (60 mL) lightly packed fresh dill, chopped

Grainy Mustard Vinaigrette

¼ cup (60 mL) freshly squeezed lemon juice

¼ cup (60 mL) extra-virgin olive oil

¼ cup (60 mL) lightly packed thinly sliced green onions (green part only)

2 tablespoons (30 mL) grainy mustard

1 tablespoon (15 mL) capers with brine

½ teaspoon (2 mL) salt

½ teaspoon (2 mL) cane sugar

Freshly cracked black pepper

1. **Boil the potatoes:** Place the potatoes in a medium pot and cover with salted water. Bring to a boil over high heat and cook until fork-tender but not too soft, 10 to 15 minutes. Drain and rinse well under cold running water. Set aside.

2. **Meanwhile, make the grainy mustard vinaigrette:** In a small blender or using a wide-mouth blending cup with a handheld immersion blender, combine the lemon juice, olive oil, and green onions. Blend until the green onions are liquified. Add the mustard, capers, salt, sugar, and pepper to taste and whisk to combine.

3. **Assemble the salad:** In a large salad bowl, combine the cooked potatoes, lentils, parsley, basil, and dill. Add the grainy mustard vinaigrette and toss to combine. Serve at room temperature or chilled. Store leftovers in an airtight container in the fridge for up to 3 days.

4
Nourishing
Soups +
Stews

Red Curry with Tofu and Vegetables

Serves 4

Gluten-Free Option

Nut-Free

Vegan

If I had to choose favourites, I would say that coconut-based curries are one of my go-to comfort meals. This flavourful and nourishing meal inspired by Thai red curries is sure to make it into your regular rotation. It's easy to adapt so that you can use the vegetables you have on hand, and it comes together quickly, even on those nights you don't feel like you have much energy to cook. Thai curries typically use fish sauce to create a more complex and flavourful base. I have substituted soy sauce—it's not a perfect swap, but it works!

1½ pounds (675 g) of your favourite vegetables (green beans, sweet potato, kabocha, or eggplant)

3 to 4 tablespoons (45 to 60 mL) vegan Thai red curry paste (I use Aroy-D; see Note)

2 cups (500 mL) canned full-fat coconut milk, divided

1 block (12 ounces/340 g) extra-firm tofu, cut into ½-inch (1 cm) cubes

2 cups (500 mL) water

2 tablespoons (30 mL) soy sauce or gluten-free tamari, plus more for seasoning

1 tablespoon (15 mL) cane sugar

½ cup (125 mL) packed fresh Thai basil leaves

Cooked jasmine rice, for serving

1. Cut the vegetables into ½-inch (1 cm) cubes. If using green beans, slice crosswise into 1-inch (2.5 cm) pieces.

2. In a large pot, combine the curry paste and ½ cup (125 mL) of the coconut milk over medium heat and cook, stirring frequently, until the mixture is thick, bubbling, and a bit darkened, 2 to 3 minutes.

3. Add the tofu and prepared vegetables, toss to coat in the curry mixture, and cook, stirring constantly, for 1 minute. Add the remaining 1½ cups (375 mL) coconut milk, water, soy sauce, and sugar and stir. Bring to a full boil over medium-high heat for 1 minute, then reduce the heat to medium-low, cover with the lid slightly ajar, and simmer until the vegetables are fork-tender, 15 to 20 minutes. Remove from the heat. Stir in the basil. Taste and adjust the soy sauce if needed.

4. Serve over cooked jasmine rice. Store leftovers in an air-tight container in the fridge for up to 4 days.

Note: Using a prepared red curry paste (most brands are vegan) makes this recipe easy to make, but it also means that if your curry paste is more heat than flavour, your curry might be bland. If the curry is not spicy enough, you can add another 1 tablespoon (15 mL) curry paste. If it's already too spicy, try adding 1 tablespoon (15 mL) soy sauce. Still missing something? Try another 1 to 2 teaspoons (5 to 10 mL) sugar.

Swaps + Stuff

For a gluten-free version, use gluten-free tamari.

Paprika Lentil Stew

Serves 6

Gluten-Free

Nut-Free

Vegan

3 tablespoons (45 mL) extra-virgin olive oil

1 large yellow onion, diced

1 sweet red pepper, diced

2 ribs celery, diced

Freshly cracked black pepper

4 cloves garlic, minced

1 can (28 ounces/798 mL) diced tomatoes

1 cup (250 mL) dried French lentils

½ cup (125 mL) Valencia or other paella-style rice

5 cups (1.25 L) water

2 tablespoons (30 mL) sweet paprika

2 teaspoons (10 mL) ground cumin

½ teaspoon (2 mL) garlic powder

½ teaspoon (2 mL) onion powder

2 bay leaves

1 teaspoon (5 mL) salt, plus more for seasoning

1 cup (250 mL) fresh curly parsley leaves and tender stems, minced

1 to 2 tablespoons (15 to 30 mL) freshly squeezed lemon juice, to taste

It's safe to say that I am firmly in my paprika phase: sweet paprika adds a wonderful depth to plant-based dishes that complements without overwhelming. And it's the perfect counterpoint to aromatic veggies, earthy cumin, and sweet tomatoes in this simple, flavourful stew that the whole family will love. It's filling without being too heavy and even more delicious the next day, as all good stews should be.

1. Heat the olive oil in a large pot over medium heat. Add the onions, sweet pepper, and celery and cook, stirring frequently, until the onions are soft and translucent, 7 to 10 minutes. Season to taste with salt and pepper.

2. Add the garlic and cook, stirring constantly, for 1 minute. Stir in the tomatoes, lentils, rice, water, sweet paprika, cumin, garlic powder, onion powder, bay leaves, and salt. Bring to a boil over medium heat and cook, uncovered, until the lentils and rice are tender, 25 to 30 minutes. As the stew thickens and bubbles, reduce the heat to medium-low if necessary to maintain a gentle boil.

3. Remove the bay leaves and discard. Stir in the parsley and 1 tablespoon (15 mL) of the lemon juice. Taste and adjust the lemon juice and salt, if needed, and add pepper. Ladle into bowls and serve. Store leftovers in an airtight container in the fridge for up to 3 days or in the freezer for up to 1 month.

Corn and Jalapeño Chowder

Serves 4

Gluten-Free Option
Nut-Free Option
Vegan

2 tablespoons (30 mL) extra-virgin olive or avocado oil

1 medium yellow onion, diced

2 ribs celery, diced

1 carrot, diced

1 poblano pepper, seeded and diced

2 medium Yukon Gold potatoes, cut into ½-inch (1 cm) cubes

3 cloves garlic, minced

1 jalapeño pepper, diced (see Note)

Freshly cracked black pepper

2 cups (500 mL) water

2 cups (500 mL) unsweetened almond milk

3 cups (750 mL) fresh or frozen corn kernels

1 can (14 ounces/398 mL) white beans (cannellini or navy)

2 teaspoons (10 mL) chicken-flavoured vegetarian stock concentrate

2 teaspoons (10 mL) onion powder

2 teaspoons (10 mL) ground cumin

1 teaspoon (5 mL) garlic powder

1 teaspoon (5 mL) dried oregano

1 teaspoon (5 mL) ground coriander

My hard-working, single mother didn't have a ton of time to cook, so growing up, we enjoyed a lot of simple home-cooked meals together. Occasionally she made corn chowder, and it felt really special. It's something I haven't made a lot of for my kids, so I thought it was high time to put my own special spin on this comforting soup. Buttery white beans, and a little bit of blending, create a rich and creamy texture with plenty of flavour—and I couldn't resist adding a bit of heat!

1. Heat the olive oil in a large pot over medium heat. Add the onions, celery, carrots, and poblano and cook, stirring occasionally, until the onions are soft and translucent, 5 to 7 minutes. Add the potatoes, garlic, and jalapeño and cook, stirring frequently, for 2 minutes. Season the vegetables with a bit of salt and pepper and stir.

2. Add the water, almond milk, corn, beans, stock concentrate, onion powder, cumin, garlic powder, oregano, coriander, and salt. Bring to a boil over high heat, then reduce the heat to medium and simmer, uncovered, until the potatoes are soft but not mushy, 20 minutes. Remove from the heat.

3. Using an immersion blender, partially purée the mixture (about half) so that it's creamy but still has plenty of texture. Stir in the nutritional yeast and butter. Taste and adjust the salt and pepper if needed. Store leftovers in an airtight container in the fridge for up to 3 days or in the freezer for up to 1 month.

recipe and ingredients continue

1 teaspoon (5 mL) salt, plus more for seasoning

1 tablespoon (15 mL) nutritional yeast

1 tablespoon (15 mL) vegan butter

Note: Always taste your jalapeño pepper for level of heat! This chowder is best with a bit of heat, so if the flesh of your pepper isn't spicy, leave the seeds in when you dice it. If the jalapeño is super spicy, remove the seeds. Cooking for wee ones? Leave the jalapeño out or add it at the table.

Swaps + Stuff

For a gluten-free version, use gluten-free stock concentrate.

For a nut-free version, use oat milk.

Cassoulet with White Beans and Swiss Chard

Serves 4

Gluten-Free Option
Nut-Free
Vegan

Calling this a cassoulet might be a bit of a stretch considering that it did not take a full day to prepare and it does not contain copious quantities of meat. But I also make black bean patties and call them burgers, so that's plant life for you. What this dish shares with cassoulet, which hails from the Occitanie region of France, are creamy, buttery white beans in a hearty stew that's slow-cooked in the oven with plenty of aromatics until it's rich and flavourful and just about the ultimate comfort food. This is Sunday afternoon cooking at its finest.

Cassoulet

1 bunch Swiss chard, leaves and stems separated

¼ cup (60 mL) extra-virgin olive oil

2 medium leeks (white and light green parts only), thinly sliced crosswise

3 ribs celery, diced

2 medium carrots, diced

4 cloves garlic, chopped

Freshly cracked black pepper

3 cans (14 ounces/398 mL each) white beans (such as butter, navy, or cannellini)

4 cups (1 L) + 1 tablespoon (15 mL) water, divided

2 tablespoons (30 mL) beef-flavoured vegetarian stock concentrate

3 sprigs fresh thyme leaves (or 1 teaspoon/5 mL dried thyme)

1 sprig (4 inches/10 cm) fresh rosemary

2 bay leaves

1 tablespoon (15 mL) dried oregano

1 teaspoon (5 mL) ground cumin

½ teaspoon (2 mL) onion powder

½ teaspoon (2 mL) garlic powder

½ teaspoon (2 mL) salt, plus more for seasoning

1 tablespoon (15 mL) arrowroot powder

1. **Start the cassoulet:** Dice the Swiss chard stems. Cut the leaves into 1-inch (2.5 cm) slices.

2. Heat the olive oil in a large soup pot over medium heat. Add the leeks, chard stems, celery, and carrots and cook, stirring frequently, until the leeks are soft and translucent, 10 to 12 minutes.

3. Add the garlic and chard leaves and cook, stirring constantly, for 1 minute. Season with salt and pepper. Add the beans, 4 cups (1 L) of the water, stock concentrate, thyme, rosemary, bay leaves, oregano, cumin, onion powder, and garlic powder and stir through. Bring to a boil over medium heat, then reduce the heat to medium-low, cover with the lid slightly ajar, and simmer, stirring occasionally, for 40 minutes or until the vegetables are tender and the stew glistens with oil. Remove the bay leaves, thyme (if using sprigs), and rosemary sprig and discard.

recipe and ingredients continue

Breadcrumb Topping

3 thin slices day-old sourdough or whole-grain bread, lightly toasted and torn into pieces

2 tablespoons (30 mL) extra-virgin olive oil

½ cup (125 mL) lightly packed fresh curly parsley leaves and tender stems, chopped

1 tablespoon (15 mL) nutritional yeast

1 clove garlic, grated on a microplane

Zest of ½ lemon

½ teaspoon (2 mL) salt

4. **Meanwhile, make the breadcrumb topping:** Toss the bread pieces into a food processor. Pulse until the mixture resembles coarse breadcrumbs with small chunks still visible.

5. In a small nonstick skillet over medium heat, add the breadcrumbs and drizzle the olive oil over top. Toast, stirring constantly, until the breadcrumbs start turning golden, 3 to 4 minutes. Turn off the heat but leave the pan on the stove top. Stir in the parsley, nutritional yeast, garlic, lemon zest, and salt and toast for 1 minute, stirring constantly, allowing the residual heat to finish toasting the breadcrumbs.

6. **Finish the cassoulet:** In a measuring cup, stir together the arrowroot and the remaining 1 tablespoon (15 mL) water until no lumps remain. Stir into the cassoulet and simmer for 10 minutes more to thicken the stew. Season with salt and pepper. Serve the cassoulet topped with breadcrumbs. Store leftovers in an airtight container in the fridge for up to 3 days.

Swaps + Stuff

For a gluten-free version, use gluten-free stock concentrate. Omit the breadcrumb topping or make the topping with gluten-free bread.

How to Meditate Without Meditating

Regulating my nervous system doesn't come naturally to me anymore. I live life at full tilt, and sometimes I can get so caught up in my to-do list that it's hard to let go. You know what's good for that? Meditation. It's like nutrition, but for anxious, stressed-out minds. When I'm meditating regularly, I'm calmer and less at the mercy of my emotions. But most of the time, my relationship with meditation feels like being diagnosed with anemia only to find that bottle of multivitamins that got pushed to the back of the pantry three years ago and thinking, Wow, *it* would have been helpful if I had remembered to take that.

I might be more like you than you think. I am a human, doing her best, trying to take care of herself. Yes, I do have a bit of an edge when it comes to nutrition knowledge, but I am also a parent and an entrepreneur and someone who stays up until midnight writing because she's behind on her deadlines, again. So I don't always live the way I would like. My toxic trait is abandoning my self-care at the very moments when I need it most. If things are chill? I'm eating my salads, moving my body, taking baths and vitamins. When things go off the rails, watch out! It could be days between workouts, vegetables, or even going outside.

There is another way, of course. I'm talking about the slow, intentional accumulation of small habits that become as second nature as brushing your teeth. They don't promise overnight nirvana, but each day they nudge you to being 1 percent better than yesterday. If this sounds good to you, pick up a copy of *Atomic Habits* by James Clear. He outlines the idea of habit stacking, which connects a new habit to an existing one to help make it automatic. We tend to be very goal oriented in nutrition, but moving toward a goal is entirely dependent on building the healthy habits you need to get you there. Because you can't white-knuckle your way through wellness for long—there is only so much energy to go around.

I've seen success with this approach in my own life. Remember when morning-routine content was a thing? People were doing the most: rising with the sun, meditating, working out, and sipping elaborate smoothies as they dry-brushed their cares away. My morning routine at the time was having my children literally pounce on me until I shook them off, peeling myself out of bed, and standing in front of the coffee maker like a zombie until that sweet, sweet elixir hit my bloodstream. Before kids, I loved starting my day with a workout, but after years of not being able to outwake my kids, I knew I needed another way to get consistent with movement. So I started tying movement to my lunch break, and now when the clock hits 11:30 a.m. it feels almost automatic to throw on my sweats and make it happen.

Even if you have a demanding schedule, there are opportunities for change. As you slump toward the coffee maker, can you fill up a glass of water and sip it as the coffee pours? Can you have your groceries delivered so you can take that precious hour on Sunday morning to go for a walk? Can you add an extra scoop of vegetables to your plate at dinner? It is these actions that will transform you over weeks and months and years without the agony of getting on or off any wagon.

Wellness isn't some to-do list that you check off daily. Because, let's be honest, not checking it off is going to cause you even more distress. Instead, think about it as a relationship and a practice. Meditation not in the cards? Can you slow your breath and notice the toothbrush moving around your mouth? That's being in the present moment, aka mindfulness. Boom, you just meditated without meditating. No time for breakfast? Instead of willing yourself to get up earlier, can you take five minutes to make overnight oats before you go to bed so you can grab and go on your way out the door the next morning? Make it so simple that you can't help but succeed. Think of how good that will feel.

In fact, cooking is a beautiful invitation to welcome more mindfulness into your life and get into the present moment. Think about it: how often have you cut yourself because you weren't paying attention? It can't be just me! Food preparation, even something as simple as overnight oats, offers you the opportunity to set an intention around your self-care and move out of your head and into the physical, tangible space of handling food. You can use the time you spend in food preparation to focus on slow, deep breathing. Or to just bring your awareness back to the colours of the plants you are cooking with, the sounds made by your knife against the cutting board. Or the onions sizzling in the pan. Are things too chaotic at 6 p.m. to create a mind spa in the kitchen? Do what I do: use noise cancelling headphones and whatever music transports you into a good headspace. For me, that's down-tempo electronic music. It's the only way I am able to develop recipes in my tiny house with family life swirling around me.

We love the grand, sweeping gestures of wellness but forget that it's what we do day in and day out that truly makes us well. Pattern over plate. Daily over monthly. Permanent over performative. That's how you get—and stay—well. And maybe, just maybe, you'll end up finally getting into meditation.

Feijoada

Serves 4

Gluten-Free Option

Nut-Free

Vegan

I grew up eating a lot of beans, feijões in Portuguese, slowly simmered until they were glistening and so flavourful. I would happily eat them by the bowlful! Here, I'm reimagining Brazilian feijoada, a meat-heavy stew of black beans, as a vegan one-pot meal. Traditionally served with rice, greens, and oranges, I've added the greens and orange juice directly into the stew, which is slowly cooked and richly flavourful. It's wonderful for Sunday dinner, and the leftovers will be delicious throughout the week.

¼ cup (60 mL) extra-virgin olive oil

2 medium yellow onions, diced

8 cloves garlic, chopped

4 vegan sausages, diced

1 tablespoon (15 mL) tomato paste

2 teaspoons (10 mL) garlic powder

1½ teaspoons (7 mL) ground cumin

¾ teaspoon (3 mL) salt

½ teaspoon (2 mL) smoked paprika

1 pound (450 g) dried black beans (about 2 cups), soaked in water for 12 to 24 hours, rinsed well, and drained

6 cups (1.5 L) water

1 tablespoon (15 mL) chicken-flavoured vegetarian stock concentrate

4 bay leaves

1 bunch collard greens or curly kale, very finely shredded

½ cup (125 mL) freshly squeezed orange juice

2 oranges, sliced, for serving (optional)

1. Heat the olive oil in a large, heavy-bottomed pot over medium heat. Add the onions and cook until very soft and translucent, 7 to 10 minutes. Add the garlic, sausage, tomato paste, garlic powder, cumin, salt, and smoked paprika and cook, stirring constantly, until glistening and fragrant, 2 to 3 minutes.

2. Add the drained beans, water, stock concentrate, and bay leaves. Bring to a boil over high heat, then reduce the heat to medium, cover with the lid slightly ajar, and simmer for 40 minutes.

3. Remove the lid and continue cooking until the beans are tender, 20 to 30 minutes. Remove the bay leaves and discard. Stir in the collard greens and cook until wilted, 2 to 3 minutes. Remove from the heat.

4. Stir in the orange juice. Taste and adjust the salt if needed. Ladle into bowls and serve with orange slices on the side, if using. Store leftovers in an airtight container in the fridge for up to 5 days. Reheat with a splash or two of water to help loosen up the stew.

Swaps + Stuff

For a gluten-free version, use gluten-free stock concentrate and omit the sausage.

Caldo Verde

Serves 4

Gluten-Free Option

Nut-Free

Vegan

This soup is proof that sometimes very simple ingredients can yield deeply satisfying results. Growing up, my avo (grandmother) made her caldo verde—green soup in Portuguese—from water without any stock or bouillon whatsoever. How she created such a flavourful soup is anyone's guess, as she refused to write down recipes. I tried it her way and then ultimately cheated a bit with some bouillon concentrate, but even my mother had to admit I got really close to recreating that magic we grew up with.

Traditionally, caldo verde is served with a few pieces of fried sausage. I've substituted vegan sausage, which is optional.

⅓ cup (75 mL) extra-virgin olive oil, plus more for frying

2 medium yellow onions, diced

1½ pounds (675 g) Yukon Gold potatoes, scrubbed and cut into ½-inch (1 cm) cubes

5 cloves garlic, finely chopped

Freshly cracked black pepper

8 cups (2 L) water

2 teaspoons (10 mL) chicken-flavoured vegetarian stock concentrate

1¼ teaspoons (6 mL) salt, plus more for seasoning

1 bay leaf

2 bunches fresh curly or Portuguese kale, destemmed and finely chopped

1 link vegan sausage, cut on the diagonal into ½-inch (1 cm) slices, for garnish (optional)

Swaps + Stuff

For a gluten-free version, use gluten-free stock concentrate and omit the sausage.

1. Heat the olive oil in a large pot over medium heat. Add the onions and cook, stirring occasionally, until soft and translucent, 5 to 7 minutes. Reduce the heat if the onions start to brown.

2. Add the potatoes and garlic and cook, stirring constantly, for 1 minute. Season with salt and pepper and stir.

3. Pour in the water and add the stock concentrate, salt, and bay leaf and bring to a boil over high heat, then reduce the heat to medium and cook, uncovered, until the potatoes are just fork-tender, 8 to 12 minutes. Remove from the heat. Discard the bay leaf.

4. Using an immersion blender, partially purée the soup (about half) for a creamy texture with chunks of potato remaining. Return to the heat, then add the kale and simmer until softened, 5 minutes. Taste and adjust the seasoning if needed.

5. Meanwhile, if garnishing with the vegan sausage, heat a drizzle of olive oil in a small skillet. Add the sausage and fry until browned, 2 to 3 minutes per side.

6. Ladle the soup into bowls and top with a few slices of sausage, if using. Store leftovers in an airtight container in the fridge for up to 4 days or in the freezer for up to 1 month.

Cream of Wild Mushroom Soup with Miso

Serves 4

Gluten-Free

Vegan

1¼ cups (300 mL) raw cashews

4 cups (1 L) water

2 tablespoons (30 mL) avocado oil

1 pound (450 g) mixed mushrooms (such as cremini, oyster, or shiitake), sliced

1 shallot, minced

4 cloves garlic, minced

Freshly cracked black pepper

2 tablespoons (30 mL) white miso

2 tablespoons (30 mL) gluten-free tamari

1½ teaspoons (7 mL) onion powder

½ teaspoon (2 mL) garlic powder

¾ teaspoon (3 mL) salt, plus more for seasoning

1 teaspoon (5 mL) pure maple syrup

Growing up, cream of mushroom soup—the one from the can—was always my favourite. Consider this my grown-up but no less comforting take on a classic, rich with umami-packed miso and tamari and loaded with a bounty of favourite mushrooms. Also, did I mention that it comes together in about thirty minutes, mostly in the blender? It's perfect for those rainy weeknights when you need a warm hug in food form. Enjoy with Black Olive and Za'atar Focaccia (page 224) as a light meal or alongside West Coast Hippie Sandwiches (page 171) for a more filling weekend lunch.

1. Combine the cashews and water in the jar of a high-speed blender. Let the cashews soak while you start cooking the vegetables.

2. Heat the avocado oil in a large nonstick skillet over medium-high heat. Add the mushrooms and cook, stirring occasionally, until browned and the water has mostly evaporated, 8 to 10 minutes. Add the shallot and garlic and cook, stirring constantly, for 1 minute. Season with salt and pepper. Remove from the heat.

3. Transfer about two thirds of the mushroom mixture into the blender with the cashews and water. Add the miso, tamari, onion powder, garlic powder, salt, and maple syrup. Purée on high speed until smooth, about 2 minutes. Pour the purée into a medium pot over medium-low heat and cook, stirring occasionally, for about 10 minutes. (Alternatively, blend on the soup setting to heat.) Taste and adjust the salt and pepper if needed.

4. Divide the remaining mushroom mixture between bowls. Ladle the soup over the mushrooms. Store leftovers in an airtight container in the fridge for up to 3 days. Separation is normal and the soup will come together when reheated.

Energizing Green Soup

Serves 4

Gluten-Free

Nut-Free Option

Vegan

Sometimes you just need an infusion of plant power, STAT. Whether you've been burning the candle at both ends or ordering takeout for far too long, this ten-minute marvel is what you make on those days when you really don't want another smoothie for lunch. Inspired by Heidi Swanson's vibrantly green blender soup, I've added some of my fave boosters: nutritional yeast for B vitamins, ginger for a troubled tummy, and a little hit of fermented foods in the form of umami-rich miso. You'll be feeling much better by the time you finish the bowl.

3 cups (750 mL) water

4 cups (1 L) packed baby spinach

1¼ cups (300 mL) partially thawed frozen green peas

1 cup (250 mL) packed fresh curly parsley leaves and tender stems

¼ cup (60 mL) raw cashews

2 tablespoons (30 mL) nutritional yeast

2 tablespoons (30 mL) white miso

2 tablespoons (30 mL) freshly squeezed lemon juice

1 tablespoon (15 mL) avocado or extra-virgin olive oil

2 cloves garlic

1 (1-inch/2.5 cm) piece fresh ginger, peeled

1½ teaspoons (7 mL) pure maple syrup

¾ teaspoon (3 mL) salt

For serving (optional)

Coconut yogurt

Chili oil

Sesame oil

1. Pour the water into a high-speed blender. Add the spinach, peas, parsley, cashews, nutritional yeast, miso, lemon juice, avocado oil, garlic, ginger, maple syrup, and salt. Blend on high speed for 2 minutes until smooth. Transfer to a medium pot over medium heat to warm. (Alternatively, blend on the soup setting to heat.)

2. Ladle the soup into bowls and garnish with your favourite toppings, if using. Store leftovers in an airtight container in the fridge for up to 3 days. Separation is normal; stir well to combine.

Swaps + Stuff

For a nut-free version, swap hemp hearts for the cashews.

Spring Minestrone

Serves 6

Gluten-Free Option
Nut-Free
Vegan

North of California, I think spring is the hardest season for local produce lovers. The root cellars are looking anemic and it's still far too cold for new growth. So when the first asparagus of the season arrive, it's time to eat them as often as humanly possible in every combination you can think of. This veggie-packed soup is a hearty, complete meal with beans and pasta that manages to welcome the arrival of spring as it warms you up, because of course it's still a little chilly outside.

3 tablespoons (45 mL) extra-virgin olive oil

2 leeks (white and light green parts only), halved lengthwise and thinly sliced

1 small zucchini, chopped

4 cloves garlic, chopped

Salt and freshly cracked black pepper

8 cups (2 L) water

2 cans (14 ounces/398 mL each) cannellini beans or navy beans

2 tablespoons (30 mL) chicken-flavoured vegetarian stock concentrate

1½ teaspoons (7 mL) dried thyme

1 teaspoon (5 mL) garlic powder

½ teaspoon (2 mL) dried oregano

1 cup (250 mL) small pasta (ditalini or cinesine)

1 pound (450 g) asparagus, trimmed and cut crosswise into 1-inch (2.5 cm) pieces

1 cup (250 mL) frozen peas

Zest of ½ lemon

2 tablespoons (30 mL) freshly squeezed lemon juice

⅓ cup (75 mL) finely chopped fresh mint leaves or curly parsley leaves, for serving (optional)

1. Heat the olive oil in a large pot over medium heat. Add the leeks, zucchini, and garlic and cook, stirring frequently, until the leeks soften, 8 to 9 minutes. Season to taste with salt and pepper.

2. Add the water, beans, stock concentrate, thyme, garlic powder, and oregano. Bring to a boil over high heat.

3. Add the pasta, reduce the heat to medium, and simmer, uncovered, for 10 minutes. Add the asparagus and peas and simmer for another 10 minutes. Reduce the heat if needed to avoid a full boil.

4. Stir in the lemon zest and lemon juice. Taste and adjust the salt if needed. Ladle into bowls and top with the mint or parsley, if using. Store leftovers in an airtight container in the fridge for up to 3 days.

Swaps + Stuff

For a gluten-free version, use gluten-free stock concentrate and gluten-free pasta.

5 Noodle Party

Soba with Miso Pecan Butter

Serves 4
Gluten-Free Option
Vegan

Soba noodles have been enjoyed in Japan for thousands of years. Made from buckwheat flour, soba noodles have such a wonderful flavour that they are commonly eaten on their own as zaru soba with just a bit of dipping sauce as an accompaniment. Since my time in Japan, I have used soba as a base for so many meals, some more traditional and others not so much, like this soba dressed with my savoury Miso Pecan Butter (page 299). Enjoy this dish as a light and simple meal or serve with Swiss Chard Goma-ae (page 61) and some steamed edamame sprinkled with shichimi togarashi as a Japan-inspired meal with friends.

1 package (8 ounces/225 g) soba noodles, gluten-free if required

½ batch Miso Pecan Butter (page 299)

Soy sauce or gluten-free tamari

2 green onions, thinly sliced on the diagonal

1 (6-inch/15 cm) piece English cucumber, diced

Shichimi togarashi or red chili flakes, for sprinkling

1. Cook the noodles according to package directions. Reserve ½ cup (125 mL) of the cooking liquid. Drain in a colander, then give the noodles a quick rinse under cool running water. Set aside.

2. In a medium bowl, mix the miso pecan butter with 2 tablespoons (30 mL) of the reserved cooking liquid until smooth. Toss with the noodles to coat. If the soba looks dry, add more cooking liquid, 2 tablespoons (30 mL) at a time, until the sauce looks glossy. Taste and adjust the seasoning with a bit of soy sauce, if needed. Top with the green onions, cucumber, and a sprinkle of shichimi togarashi or chili flakes. Store leftovers in an airtight container in the fridge for up to 3 days. Reheat with a splash of water to rehydrate the sauce.

Swaps + Stuff
For a gluten-free version, use gluten-free soba noodles and gluten-free tamari.

Pasta al Limone

Serves 4

Gluten-Free Option

Vegan

Some things in life are constant, like my love of a good cream sauce. Pasta al limone is a classic Italian pasta, and I've given this comforting dish a vegan twist by using a cashew cream base and substituting nutritional yeast for Parmesan cheese for a hit of umami. I love curling up with a bowl of this pasta on a cold night, all on its own, but it would also be delicious served with Garlic-Sautéed Rapini (page 142).

1 cup (250 mL) raw cashews

1 cup (250 mL) water

1 tablespoon (15 mL) nutritional yeast

1 teaspoon (5 mL) salt

½ teaspoon (2 mL) garlic powder

Zest of ½ lemon

¼ cup (60 mL) freshly squeezed lemon juice

1 package (12 ounces/340 g) spaghetti

For serving (optional)

Red chili flakes

Nutritional yeast

1. **Make the sauce:** In a high-speed blender, combine the cashews, water, nutritional yeast, salt, garlic powder, and lemon zest. Blend on high speed until smooth, about 1 minute. Add the lemon juice and blend on low speed for 20 seconds. Set aside.

2. **Cook the pasta:** Cook the pasta according to package directions. Reserve ½ cup (125 mL) of the cooking liquid. Drain in a colander, then give the noodles a quick rinse under cool running water. Return to the pot.

3. **Assemble:** Pour the sauce over the pasta. Add ¼ cup (60 mL) of the reserved cooking liquid and toss to coat. If the pasta looks dry, add a bit more cooking liquid until the sauce looks glossy.

4. Divide the pasta between bowls. Sprinkle with a bit of chili flakes and nutritional yeast, if desired. Store leftovers in an airtight container in the fridge for up to 3 days. Reheat with a splash of water to rehydrate the sauce.

Swaps + Stuff

For a gluten-free version, use gluten-free pasta.

An Easy, Cozy Lasagna

Serves 8
Gluten-Free Option
Nut-Free Option
Vegan

When you go plant-based, it takes time to find your groove with creating new traditions during special occasions. For our family, that meal was Christmas Eve dinner—until I started making this lasagna. It's all decadence, with plenty of cashew cream bechamel and melty vegan shreds, but also quite simple to make as far as lasagnas go! I use jarred sauce and oven-ready noodles. Plus, it's much easier to blend up a cashew cream than to make bechamel over the stove. Everyone in my family gobbles this up, despite my being the only plant person in the house.

Vegetable Mixture

2 tablespoons (30 mL) extra-virgin olive or avocado oil

1 pound (450 g) cremini mushrooms, sliced

1 yellow onion, diced

1 package (12 ounces/340 g) veggie ground (optional)

4 cloves garlic, chopped

6 cups (1.5 L) packed baby spinach

Salt and freshly cracked black pepper

Cashew Cream Bechamel

1½ cups (375 mL) raw cashews

1¼ cups (300 mL) water

1 teaspoon (5 mL) salt

1 teaspoon (5 mL) garlic powder

1 teaspoon (5 mL) nutritional yeast

1. Preheat the oven to 375°F (190°C).

2. **Prepare the vegetable mixture:** Heat the olive oil in a large nonstick skillet over medium heat. Add the mushrooms and onions and cook, stirring occasionally, until the onions are soft and translucent and the mushrooms have released water and are starting to brown, 10 to 12 minutes.

3. Add the veggie ground (if using), garlic, and spinach (in batches, if needed) and cook, stirring constantly, until the spinach wilts, 1 to 2 minutes. Season with salt and pepper. Remove from the heat and set aside.

4. **Make the cashew cream bechamel:** In a high-speed blender, combine the cashews, water, salt, garlic powder, and nutritional yeast. Blend on high speed until creamy, about 1 minute.

recipe and ingredients continue

For assembly

1 jar (24 ounces/680 g) of your favourite marinara sauce (I use Rao's)

12 oven-ready wheat or gluten-free lasagna noodles

½ pound (225 g) meltable grated vegan cheese

5. **Assemble the lasagna:** Spread one third of the marinara sauce into the bottom of a 13 × 9-inch (3.5 L) baking dish. Layer 4 noodles over the sauce. Spread with half of the cashew cream and half of the vegetable mixture. Pour another third of the marinara sauce over top. Add the next layer of 4 noodles and top with the remaining cashew cream and vegetable mixture. Top with the remaining 4 noodles, the remaining marinara sauce, and the grated cheese. Cover the pan with foil and bake for 30 minutes. Remove the foil and bake for another 15 minutes, until the lasagna is bubbling at the sides. Let sit for 10 minutes before serving. Store leftovers in an airtight container in the fridge for up to 3 days.

Swaps + Stuff

For a nut-free version, swap raw sunflower seeds (soaked in water overnight and drained) for the cashews.

For a gluten-free version, use gluten-free lasagna noodles.

Spicy Tomato Pasta with Capers and Olives

Serves 4

Gluten-Free Option

Nut-Free

Vegan

Last time I checked, olives were a plant and that's all the justification I need to eat more of these salty, tangy orbs. This spunky, boldly flavoured pasta is my vegan take on a traditional pasta dish hailing from Naples, Italy. Nutritional yeast and extra capers lend an umami-rich, briny note to this rich garlic-spiked tomato sauce that will leave you wanting more. Never one to leave well enough alone, I've added roasted chickpeas for extra crunch.

Roasted Chickpeas

1 can (14 ounces/398 mL) chickpeas, rinsed and drained

1 tablespoon (15 mL) avocado oil

1 teaspoon (5 mL) nutritional yeast

½ teaspoon (2 mL) salt

½ teaspoon (2 mL) garlic powder

Spicy Tomato Pasta with Capers and Olives

1 pound (450 g) of your favourite shape pasta (I like rigatoni or fusilli)

3 tablespoons (45 mL) extra-virgin olive oil

5 cloves garlic, chopped

½ teaspoon (2 mL) red chili flakes

1 can (14 ounces/398 mL) San Marzano tomatoes

⅓ cup (75 mL) pitted Kalamata olives, chopped

¼ cup (60 mL) drained capers, chopped

2 tablespoons (30 mL) nutritional yeast

1 tablespoon (15 mL) caper brine

Salt

1. **Roast the chickpeas:** Preheat the oven to 400°F (200°C). Line a small baking sheet with parchment paper.

2. Scatter the chickpeas on the prepared baking sheet. Toss with the avocado oil, nutritional yeast, salt, and garlic powder. Spread evenly on the baking sheet and roast until golden brown and crispy, 25 to 30 minutes.

3. **Meanwhile, cook the pasta:** Cook the pasta 1 minute less than on package directions. Reserve 1 cup (250 mL) of the cooking liquid. Drain the pasta, but don't rinse it.

4. **Make the sauce and finish:** Heat the olive oil in a medium skillet over medium heat. Add the garlic and chili flakes and cook, stirring frequently, until fragrant and golden, 3 to 4 minutes. Watch closely so the garlic doesn't brown.

5. Using your hands, crush the tomatoes in a small bowl. Pour the crushed tomatoes and all their juices into the skillet. Stir in the olives and capers and cook, uncovered, stirring occasionally, until the sauce has thickened and is glistening, 14 to 16 minutes.

recipe continues

6. Add the cooked pasta, nutritional yeast, caper brine, and ¼ cup (60 mL) of the reserved cooking liquid. Cook for 2 minutes, tossing often to allow the pasta to absorb some flavour, until al dente. If drying out, add a bit more cooking liquid and stir. Taste and adjust salt if needed. (I like to add another ¼ teaspoon/1 mL salt.) Divide the pasta between bowls and top with the roasted chickpeas. Store leftover pasta and chickpeas in separate airtight containers in the fridge for up to 3 days.

Swaps + Stuff

For a gluten-free version, use gluten-free pasta.

Avocado Pesto Pasta

Serves 4

Gluten-Free Option
Nut-Free
Vegan

Is there anything an avocado can't do? I think of pesto more as a formula than a recipe. You need something herby—here, that's traditional basil and not so traditional green onion—plus a nut or seed, an allium like garlic, a little hit of umami—which I add in the form of nutritional yeast instead of Parmesan cheese—and finally some silky oil or fat like avocado to bind it all together. Pesto is flexible, so feel free to change up this recipe based on the nuts or seeds you have in your pantry. It will be delicious just the same.

12 ounces (340 g) of your favourite long pasta (such as spaghetti or fettucine)

Pesto

4 green onions, roughly chopped

1 cup (250 mL) packed fresh basil leaves

¼ cup (60 mL) raw pumpkin seeds

1 large ripe avocado, pitted and peeled

1 clove garlic, crushed or grated on a microplane

2 tablespoons (30 mL) freshly squeezed lemon juice

2 tablespoons (30 mL) nutritional yeast

1 teaspoon (5 mL) garlic powder

1 teaspoon (5 mL) salt, plus more for seasoning

Pinch of red chili flakes or lots of freshly cracked black pepper

1. **Start the pasta:** Cook the pasta according to package directions. Reserve 1 cup (250 mL) of the cooking liquid. Drain in a colander, then give the noodles a quick rinse under cool running water. Return to the pot.

2. **Meanwhile, make the pesto:** In a small food processor, combine the green onions, basil, and pumpkin seeds. Pulse until finely chopped. Add the avocado, garlic, lemon juice, nutritional yeast, garlic powder, salt, and chili flakes and blend to a mostly smooth paste. There will still be some texture from the pumpkin seeds.

3. **Assemble:** Toss the pesto with the pasta, thinning as needed with the reserved cooking liquid. The pesto should look glossy. Taste and adjust the salt and chili flakes if needed. Store leftovers in an airtight container in the fridge for up to 3 days. To reheat, combine the pasta with a splash of water in a medium nonstick skillet over medium heat until warmed through.

Swaps + Stuff

For a gluten-free version, use gluten-free pasta.

Salad Noodles

Serves 4
Gluten-Free
Low-FODMAP Option
Nut-Free
Vegan

Inspired by Vietnamese bun (rice vermicelli) dishes, this refreshing noodle bowl piles on plenty of veggies and is lavished in a nuoc cham-inspired dressing for a fresh and flavourful meal that comes together quickly and is so lovely on a hot day. Noodles are the base, but vegetables make it a party. So don't call this a noodle salad—these are salad noodles.

Salad

2 cups (500 mL) frozen shelled edamame

½ pound (225 g) glass noodles or rice vermicelli

1 cup (250 mL) lo bok or daikon radish, finely sliced into rounds or matchsticks

1 sweet yellow pepper, thinly sliced

½ cup (125 mL) packed fresh mint leaves, thinly sliced

½ cup (125 mL) packed fresh cilantro leaves

Nuoc Cham–Inspired Dressing

½ cup (125 mL) freshly squeezed lime juice

2 tablespoons (30 mL) cane sugar

½ cup (125 mL) water

2 tablespoons (30 mL) rice vinegar

2 tablespoons (30 mL) soy sauce or gluten-free tamari

1 tablespoon (15 mL) avocado oil

¾ teaspoon (3 mL) salt

1 clove garlic, grated on a microplane

1 fresh Thai red chili, sliced (or chili garlic hot sauce)

1. **Start the salad:** Bring a large pot of water to a boil over high heat. Add the edamame and cook for 2 minutes. Add the noodles to the pot with the edamame and cook according to package directions. Drain in a colander, then give the noodles a quick rinse under cool running water. Transfer the edamame and noodles to a large shallow serving bowl.

2. **Make the nuoc cham–inspired dressing:** In a small bowl, whisk together the lime juice and sugar until the sugar is mostly dissolved. Whisk in the water, rice vinegar, soy sauce, avocado oil, salt, garlic, and Thai chili to taste.

3. **Assemble the salad:** In the large shallow serving bowl, arrange the radish, sweet pepper, mint, and cilantro on top of the noodles and edamame. Serve with the nuoc cham–inspired dressing on the side for drizzling generously over the noodles. Store the dressing and salad in separate air-tight containers in the fridge for up to 2 days.

Swaps + Stuff

For a low-FODMAP version, use rice vermicelli and swap a green pepper for the yellow pepper. Omit the garlic from the dressing.

Roasted Fennel and Chickpea Pasta with Harissa Cream

I'm all for simplifying but admit that most of the time I take a more is more approach to food. More texture. More flavour. More vegetables! This pasta checks all the boxes. A cashew cream sauce is whipped up in the blender with fiery harissa, a Tunisian spice paste that is one of my favourite ingredients. The chickpeas roast up crisp while the fennel mellows and softens in the oven. And it all comes together in about 45 minutes.

Serves 6

Gluten-Free

Nut-Free Option

Vegan

Roasted Fennel and Chickpeas

2 small fennel bulbs

2 cans (14 ounces/398 mL each) chickpeas, rinsed and drained

3 tablespoons (45 mL) avocado oil

1½ teaspoons (7 mL) ground coriander

1 teaspoon (5 mL) garlic powder

¾ teaspoon (3 mL) salt

Freshly cracked black pepper

1 pound (450 g) gluten-free pasta

Zest of 1 lemon, for garnish

Harissa Cream Sauce

1¼ cups (300 mL) raw cashews

1 cup (250 mL) water

1 tablespoon (15 mL) nutritional yeast

1 tablespoon (15 mL) harissa paste, plus more to taste

4 teaspoons (20 mL) freshly squeezed lemon juice

1 clove garlic

1 teaspoon (5 mL) salt

Swaps + Stuff

For a nut-free version, swap raw sunflower seeds (soaked in water overnight and drained) for the cashews.

1. **Roast the fennel and chickpeas:** Preheat the oven to 400°F (200°C). Line a baking sheet with parchment paper.

2. Working on a cutting board, trim the fennel bulbs. Then, cut the bulbs in half, core, and cut lengthwise into ⅓-inch (8 mm) thick slices. Lightly chop the fronds and reserve for garnish. Place the fennel and chickpeas on the prepared baking sheet. Drizzle with the avocado oil and sprinkle the coriander, garlic powder, salt, and pepper to taste over top. Toss well to coat. Spread evenly on the baking sheet and bake, stirring halfway through, until the chickpeas are golden and the fennel is caramelized and fork-tender, 35 to 40 minutes.

3. **Start the pasta:** Meanwhile, cook the pasta according to package directions. Reserve 1 cup (250 mL) of the cooking liquid. Drain in a colander, then give the noodles a quick rinse under cool running water. Transfer to a large serving bowl.

4. **Make the harissa cream sauce:** In a high-speed blender, combine the cashews, water, nutritional yeast, harissa, lemon juice, garlic, and salt. Blend on high speed for 1 minute until smooth.

5. **Assemble:** Pour the harissa cream sauce over the pasta and toss, adding a little bit of cooking liquid if needed to create a glossy sauce. Top with the fennel and chickpea mixture. Garnish with the reserved fennel fronds and lemon zest. Store leftovers in an airtight container in the fridge for up to 3 days.

Chili Oil Ramen with Greens

Serves 4

Gluten-Free Option
Nut-Free Option
Vegan

After you try this incredibly fast and flavourful meal packed with greens, I am sure it will become a constant craving. Making chili oil—or noodles—this way is nothing new: chili oil is a common feature in Sichuan cuisine. And you po mian is a noodle dish hailing from the Shaanxi province of China in which screaming-hot oil is poured over chili-spiked noodles. My vegan take on this dish adds salted peanuts for crunch; if you want a bit of protein, try adding some simple pan-fried tofu.

Chili Oil

6 green onions, thinly sliced on the diagonal

3 tablespoons (45 mL) soy sauce or gluten-free tamari, plus more for seasoning

1 tablespoon (15 mL) minced peeled fresh ginger

2 cloves garlic, crushed or grated on a microplane

1 teaspoon (5 mL) red chili flakes

1 teaspoon (5 mL) cane sugar

¼ cup (60 mL) avocado oil

Ramen with Greens

1½ pounds (675 g) gai lan or choy sum, trimmed and cut into 1-inch (2.5 cm) lengths

1 teaspoon (5 mL) sesame oil

1 teaspoon (5 mL) soy sauce or gluten-free tamari

4 bricks (3½ ounces/100 g each) ramen noodles

¼ cup (60 mL) salted peanuts, chopped

1. **Start the chili oil:** In a large heatproof serving bowl, stir together the green onions, soy sauce, ginger, garlic, chili flakes, and sugar. Set aside.

2. **Prepare the ramen with greens:** Bring a large pot of water to boil over high heat. Add the gai lan and cook until tender-crisp, 3 to 5 minutes. Using a slotted spoon, scoop out the gai lan and transfer to a medium bowl. Toss with the sesame oil and soy sauce. Set aside. Keep the pot of water boiling.

3. To the pot, add the ramen noodles and cook according to package directions. Drain in a colander, then give the noodles a quick rinse under cool running water. Set aside.

4. **Finish the chili oil and assemble:** Heat the avocado oil in a small pot over medium heat until shimmering, 3 to 5 minutes. The oil is ready when a piece of green onion dropped in the hot oil sizzles. Carefully pour the hot oil over the green onion mixture in the serving bowl and stir to mix.

5. Add the ramen noodles to the hot chili oil and toss to coat. Top with the gai lan and sprinkle with the peanuts. Store leftovers in an airtight container in the fridge for up to 2 days. They are delicious cold.

Swaps + Stuff

For a gluten-free version, use gluten-free ramen noodles and tamari.

For a nut-free version, omit the peanuts.

Mushroom Stroganoff

Serves 4

Gluten-Free Option
Nut-Free
Vegan

Pasta. Mushrooms. Creamy sauce. What more could you want? This vegan take on beef stroganoff, a dish featuring a sour cream and mustard sauce that has its origins in nineteenth-century Russia, strays a fair bit from its traditional form but is absolutely as savoury and delicious. This looks like a lot of ingredients, but it's mostly spices and condiments—and if you buy sliced mushrooms, it comes together quickly!

1 cup (250 mL) water

2 tablespoons (30 mL) cornstarch

12 ounces (340 g) your favourite shape pasta (I like bow tie)

2 tablespoons (30 mL) extra-virgin olive oil

1¼ pounds (565 g) cremini mushrooms, sliced

1 large shallot, finely chopped

4 cloves garlic, minced

Salt and freshly cracked black pepper

2 cups (500 mL) unsweetened oat milk

2 tablespoons (30 mL) soy sauce or gluten-free tamari

1 tablespoon (15 mL) vegan Worcestershire sauce, gluten-free if required

1 teaspoon (5 mL) beef-flavoured vegetarian stock concentrate

1 tablespoon (15 mL) nutritional yeast

2 teaspoons (10 mL) sweet paprika

1 teaspoon (5 mL) dried thyme

1½ teaspoons (7 mL) onion powder

2 tablespoons (30 mL) Dijon mustard

½ cup (125 mL) fresh dill, chopped

1. In a small bowl, whisk together the water and cornstarch. Set aside.

2. Cook the pasta according to package directions. Drain in a colander, then give the noodles a quick rinse under cool running water. Set aside.

3. Heat the olive oil in a deep large skillet or pot over medium-high heat. Add the mushrooms and cook, stirring occasionally, until the released moisture evaporates and the mushrooms are browned, 7 to 10 minutes. Reduce the heat to medium.

4. Add the shallot and garlic and cook, stirring constantly, until the shallot softens. Season with salt and pepper.

5. Stir in the oat milk, cornstarch mixture, soy sauce, Worcestershire sauce, stock concentrate, nutritional yeast, sweet paprika, thyme, and onion powder. Cook, uncovered, stirring occasionally, until the mixture thickens, 7 to 10 minutes. Remove from the heat. Stir in the mustard and dill. Taste and adjust the salt and pepper if needed. (I usually add another ¼ teaspoon/1 mL of salt and plenty of pepper.)

6. Divide the pasta between bowls and ladle the mushroom sauce over top. Store the pasta and sauce in separate airtight containers in the fridge for up to 3 days.

Swaps + Stuff

For a gluten-free version, use gluten-free Worcestershire sauce, tamari, stock concentrate, and pasta.

6 Stuff on Bread

Cumin Lime Black Bean Burgers

Makes 6 patties

Gluten-Free Option
Nut-Free
Vegan

1 cup (250 mL) packed fresh
    cilantro leaves and tender
    stems

½ medium yellow onion, roughly
    chopped

½ cup (125 mL) gluten-free old-
    fashioned rolled oats

4 cloves garlic

2 cans (14 ounces/398 mL each)
    black beans, rinsed and
    drained

¼ cup (60 mL) ground flaxseed

2 teaspoons (10 mL) ground cumin

1 teaspoon (5 mL) onion powder

1 teaspoon (5 mL) salt

½ teaspoon (2 mL) garlic powder

½ teaspoon (2 mL) ground
    coriander

Juice of 1 lime (about
    2 tablespoons/30 mL)

1 tablespoon (15 mL) extra-virgin
    olive or avocado oil, plus more
    for cooking

For serving

Hamburger buns, whole-grain or
    gluten-free

Vegan mayonnaise

Sliced or smashed avocado

Pickled Red Onions (page 292)

Spicy Cilantro Garlic Sauce
    (page 293)

I've got all sorts of opinions, particularly when it comes to veggie burgers. If I'm making a burger from scratch, it's going to be the soft and squishy kind. No dry veggie burgers for this gal! I am also firmly committed to burgers that are weeknight doable. No additional cooking, just blend, pat, and fry. Serve these with Carrot and Parsnip Fries with Tahini Garlic Aioli (page 73) to double down on the plant power.

1. In a food processor, combine the cilantro, onions, rolled oats, and garlic and pulse until finely chopped. Add the black beans, flaxseed, cumin, onion powder, salt, garlic powder, coriander, lime juice, and olive oil. Pulse 6 to 8 times until about half the mixture resembles a paste, but you can still see plenty of texture. Be careful not to purée the whole mixture or the burgers will not stick together.

2. Heat a large nonstick skillet over medium heat. Scoop a generous ⅓ cup (75 mL) of the bean mixture and flatten it into a patty in the pan to ¾ inch (2 cm) thick and 3 to 4 inches (8 to 10 cm) wide. Cook, in batches if needed, until a brown crust forms on the bottom, 4 to 5 minutes. If browning too fast, reduce the heat so the burgers have time to cook through without burning on the bottom. Carefully flip and cook for another 4 to 5 minutes until brown on the other side. (You can freeze uncooked patties, stored between layers of parchment paper in a resealable plastic freezer bag, for up to 1 month. Cook from frozen, until cooked through and golden brown, 7 to 8 minutes per side.)

3. To serve, slice open the buns and spread some mayonnaise on the bottom half of each and top with a patty, sliced or smashed avocado, and pickled red onions. Spread some of the spicy cilantro garlic sauce on each of the bun tops, then arrange them on top of the pickled red onions.

Swaps + Stuff

For a gluten-free version, use gluten-free buns.

Pizza with Balsamic Tomatoes, Soft Cheese, and Corn Nuts

I love a pizza night, but I have a confession to make. I almost never make my own dough! Instead, I get a sourdough-based dough from my favourite bakery, Flourist, and that frees me up to spend a little extra effort on the toppings. The tangy, balsamic-laced tomatoes are packed with flavour and pair well with a soft, chevre-style cashew cheese and salty, crunchy corn nuts. Yes, corn nuts! I'm obsessed with this childhood fave and think they're due for a comeback.

Makes 2 medium pizzas

Gluten-Free Option
Nut-Free Option
Vegan

2 prepared pizza crusts (or enough fresh pizza dough to make two 14-inch/35 cm pizzas)

1 tablespoon (15 mL) extra-virgin olive oil, plus more for brushing

1 small red onion, sliced into thin half-moons

2 pints (4 cups/1 L) cherry tomatoes, halved

4 cloves garlic, chopped

¼ cup (60 mL) balsamic vinegar

1 tablespoon (15 mL) brown sugar

½ teaspoon (2 mL) salt

Freshly cracked black pepper

1 cup (250 mL) semi-soft cashew cheese or Herbed Cashew Cheese (page 297), crumbled

½ cup (125 mL) corn nuts, crushed

¾ cup (175 mL) fresh basil leaves, thinly sliced

Red chili flakes

1. If you are using a pizza stone, place it on the middle rack of the oven. Preheat the oven to 450°F (230°C).

2. If using pizza dough, prepare according to package directions.

3. Heat the olive oil in a large skillet over medium heat. Add the red onions and cook, stirring occasionally, until softened, 5 to 7 minutes. Add the tomatoes and garlic and cook, stirring occasionally, until the tomatoes start to soften and release their juices, about 5 minutes.

4. Stir in the balsamic vinegar, brown sugar, and salt and cook until saucy and the liquid has mostly evaporated, 5 to 7 minutes. Season with lots of black pepper. Remove from the heat.

5. Place the pizza crusts, or rolled-out pizza dough, on a sheet of parchment paper if using a pizza stone or on a sheet of foil. Brush the crusts with a little olive oil.

recipe continues

6. Divide the balsamic tomato mixture between the crusts and spread evenly, leaving a 1-inch (2.5 cm) border of exposed dough. Bake the pizza crusts one at a time. Slide the parchment with the crust or dough onto the pizza stone (or the foil directly onto the oven rack). Bake according to package directions or 8 to 10 minutes. Repeat to bake the remaining pizza crust. Remove from the oven and top with dollops of cashew cheese. Sprinkle the corn nuts and basil on top. Cut the pizzas into wedges and serve with chili flakes. Store leftover balsamic tomato mixture in an airtight container in the fridge for up to 5 days. Store leftover pizza tightly wrapped in the fridge for up to 3 days.

Swaps + Stuff

For a gluten-free version, use gluten-free pizza crusts or pizza dough.

For a nut-free version, swap shredded nut-free cheese for the cashew cheese and sprinkle on the pizza just before baking.

Sweet and Spicy Lentil Sloppy Joes with Pickle Slaw

Growing up, we ate a solid fifty-fifty mix of traditional Portuguese food and food my grandmother discovered in the 1960s. However, sloppy joes were not one of these discoveries, so they became firmly entrenched in my mind as food that people only ate on TV shows. I hope this sweet and spicy lentil variety does my childhood Hollywood dreams justice! I highly recommend that you serve them on a soft-style bun to better cradle these lentils, and don't skip the slaw. It cuts the richness of the dish and adds some heat.

Serves 6

Gluten-Free Option

Nut-Free

Vegan

Sloppy Joe Mix

1 cup (250 mL) dried French lentils, rinsed (or 2½ cups/625 mL cooked lentils)

2 tablespoons (30 mL) extra-virgin olive or avocado oil

1 small yellow onion, diced

1 sweet red pepper, diced

3 cloves garlic, minced

2 teaspoons (10 mL) onion powder

2 teaspoons (10 mL) chili powder

1 teaspoon (5 mL) ground cumin

½ teaspoon (2 mL) garlic powder

½ teaspoon (2 mL) smoked paprika

1 cup (250 mL) strained tomatoes (passata)

½ cup (125 mL) water

2 tablespoons (30 mL) pure maple syrup

2 tablespoons (30 mL) blackstrap molasses

1 tablespoon (15 mL) apple cider vinegar

1 teaspoon (5 mL) vegan Worcestershire sauce

1. **Cook the lentils:** Place the dried lentils in a small saucepan. Pour in enough water to cover the lentils by 3 inches (8 cm). Bring to a boil over high heat, then reduce the heat to medium, cover with the lid slightly ajar, and cook until tender yet still a bit firm, 12 to 16 minutes. Drain in a fine-mesh sieve and rinse under cool running water. Drain again and set aside.

2. **Prepare the sloppy joe mix:** Heat the olive oil in a large nonstick skillet over medium heat. Add the onions and sweet pepper and cook, stirring occasionally, until the onions are very soft and translucent, 7 to 10 minutes.

3. Add the garlic, onion powder, chili powder, cumin, garlic powder, and smoked paprika and cook for 1 minute, stirring frequently so the garlic doesn't burn.

recipe and ingredients continue

¾ teaspoon (3 mL) salt

¼ to ½ teaspoon (1 to 2 mL) red chili flakes, depending on level of heat desired

Freshly cracked black pepper

Pickle Slaw

2 tablespoons (30 mL) apple cider vinegar

1 teaspoon (5 mL) hot sauce (I use Valentina extra hot), plus more for serving

¼ teaspoon (1 mL) cane sugar

¼ teaspoon (1 mL) garlic powder

¼ teaspoon (1 mL) salt

2 cups (500 mL) packed shredded red cabbage or coleslaw mix

1 medium dill pickle (or 2 to 3 bread and butter pickles), cut into thin matchsticks

For serving

6 vegan potato-style buns or soft gluten-free buns

Vegan mayonnaise

4. Stir in the cooked lentils, strained tomatoes, water, maple syrup, molasses, apple cider vinegar, Worcestershire sauce, salt, and chili flakes. Simmer, uncovered, for 10 minutes over medium-low heat to allow the flavours to meld and the mixture to thicken. Taste and adjust the salt and pepper if needed.

5. **Make the pickle slaw:** In a medium bowl, whisk together the apple cider vinegar, hot sauce, sugar, garlic powder, and salt. Add the shredded cabbage and pickle and toss to combine. Set aside.

6. **Assemble the sloppy joes:** Slice open the buns and thinly spread some mayonnaise on the bottom half of each. Top with a scoop of lentil mixture and some pickle slaw. Finish the sloppy joes with the bun tops. Serve with hot sauce on the side. Store leftover sloppy joe mix in an airtight container in the fridge for up to 3 days or in the freezer for up to 1 month.

Swaps + Stuff

For a gluten-free version, use gluten-free Worcestershire sauce and gluten-free buns.

West Coast Hippie Sandwiches

Makes 4 sandwiches

Gluten-Free Option

Nut-Free Option

Vegan

8 slices grainy or gluten-free bread, toasted

Vegan mayonnaise

1 avocado, pitted, peeled, and sliced

1 cup (250 mL) thinly sliced English cucumber

¼ red onion, thinly sliced

1 cup (250 mL) broccoli or alfalfa sprouts

Flaky sea salt and freshly cracked black pepper

½ cup (125 mL) Herbed Cashew Cheese (page 297) or other semi-firm cashew cheese

I am, as they say, of a certain age, so I can remember heading to The Sandwich Tree in the food court as a kid for sandwiches piled high with cream cheese and sprouts. Sprouts were the epitome of West Coast hippie food and with good reason: they're superpowered plant foods, packed with phytochemicals far beyond their mature veggie counterparts. This sandwich is my take on that retro treat and might just inspire you to start growing sprouts at home so you can live out your crunchy granola dreams.

1. Place the slices of toasted bread on a cutting board.

2. Thinly spread some mayonnaise on 4 slices of the bread. Layer each with a few slices of avocado, cucumbers, red onions, and sprouts. Sprinkle to taste with flaky sea salt and pepper.

3. Spread about 2 tablespoons (30 mL) of the herbed cashew cheese on each of the remaining 4 slices of bread and close the sandwiches.

Swaps + Stuff

For a gluten-free version, use gluten-free bread.

For a nut-free version, swap a nut-free vegan cream cheese for the cashew cheese.

Brussels Sprout Grilled Cheese Sandwiches

Makes 4 sandwiches

Gluten-Free Option

Nut-Free

Vegan

1 tablespoon (15 mL) avocado oil

½ pound (225 g) Brussels sprouts, finely shredded

½ shallot, minced

1 clove garlic, finely chopped

1 tablespoon (15 mL) grainy mustard

1 teaspoon (5 mL) pure maple syrup

¼ teaspoon (1 mL) salt

Freshly cracked black pepper

For assembly

8 slices sprouted grain, sourdough, or gluten-free bread

Vegan butter

4 slices meltable vegan cheese

Back in my vegetarian days, I made a mean grilled cheese. And going vegan doesn't mean that my grilled cheese days are over! I love dressing them up with new flavours and textures, like savoury Brussels sprouts. Brussels sprouts are easily one of my favourite vegetables, and when shredded they take on a delicate flavour and texture that goes so well with sharp, grainy mustard and your favourite vegan cheese. Because you're never too old for a really good grilled cheese sandwich.

1. **Make the Brussels sprout mixture:** Heat the avocado oil in a medium nonstick skillet over medium heat. Add the Brussels sprouts, shallots, and garlic and cook, stirring frequently, until the sprouts are softened and browned, about 5 minutes. Remove from the heat.

2. Add the mustard, maple syrup, salt, and pepper to taste and toss to combine.

3. **Assemble and cook:** Place the slices of bread on a cutting board and thinly spread butter on the top side of each. Heat a large nonstick skillet over medium-low heat. When the skillet is hot, place 2 slices of bread, butter side down, in the pan and top each with a slice of cheese and a quarter of the Brussels sprout mixture. Top each with a remaining slice of bread, butter side up, and cook until golden brown on the bottom, 3 to 4 minutes. Flip the sandwiches and cook until the other sides are golden brown on the bottom, another 3 to 4 minutes. Press down on the sandwiches with a spatula in the last minute of cooking to help with browning and to melt the cheese. Repeat to cook the remaining 2 sandwiches. (Alternatively, you can cook the sandwiches using a panini press or waffle iron.) Store leftover Brussels sprout mixture in an airtight container in the fridge for up to 2 days.

Swaps + Stuff

For a gluten-free version, use gluten-free bread.

Rajas Con Crema

Serves 4

Gluten-Free Option

Nut-Free Option

Vegan

I've included this recipe by request from Gabriel Cabrera, *Plant Magic*'s incredible photographer, who doesn't eat dairy and was missing the rajas con crema he grew up with in Mexico. Rajas refers to strips of poblano peppers, a mild pepper, that are lavished with a creamy sauce. Creating a vegan version of this dish meant swapping cashew cream for dairy, but otherwise it's close to the original. Poblano peppers are grilled until they're soft and the skin slips off easily, then cooked with corn, onions, and garlic in a heavenly creamy sauce.

4 poblano peppers

1 tablespoon (15 mL) avocado oil

1 small white onion, thinly sliced into half-moons

1 cup (250 mL) fresh or frozen corn kernels

1 teaspoon (5 mL) garlic powder

½ teaspoon (2 mL) onion powder

½ teaspoon (2 mL) ground cumin

½ teaspoon (2 mL) salt

1 tablespoon (15 mL) freshly squeezed lemon juice

Cashew Cream

¾ cup (175 mL) raw cashews

¾ cup (175 mL) water

2 tablespoons (30 mL) nutritional yeast

½ teaspoon (2 mL) salt, plus more for seasoning

½ teaspoon (2 mL) garlic powder

For serving

8 small tortillas, warmed (I use blue corn tortillas)

Hot sauce (I use Valentina extra hot)

Lime wedges

1. **Grill the poblanos:** Preheat the grill to medium (400° to 450°F/200° to 230°C).

2. Place the poblanos on the grill and cook until blistered on all sides, about 15 minutes total. Transfer to a plate and let sit until cool enough to handle.

3. Peel the poblanos and remove the stem and seeds. Slice the poblanos into thin strips.

4. **Make the poblano and vegetable mixture:** Heat the avocado oil in a medium skillet over medium heat. Add the onions and cook, stirring occasionally, until soft and translucent, 5 to 7 minutes. Add the corn, poblanos, garlic powder, onion powder, cumin, and salt and cook, stirring frequently, until the corn is heated through, 2 to 3 minutes. Remove from the heat.

5. **Make the cashew cream:** In a high-speed blender, combine the cashews, water, nutritional yeast, salt, and garlic powder. Blend on high speed until smooth, 1 to 2 minutes.

6. **Assemble:** Pour the cashew cream over the vegetable mixture. Stir in the lemon juice. Taste and adjust the salt if needed. Divide the creamy vegetable mixture between the warmed tortillas and serve with hot sauce and lime wedges. Store leftover filling in an airtight container in the fridge for up to 3 days. Reheat with a splash of water to rehydrate the sauce.

Swaps + Stuff

For a gluten-free version, use gluten-free tortillas.

For a nut-free version, swap sunflower seeds for the cashews. Soak the sunflower seeds in water overnight. Drain when ready to make the sauce.

On Potato Chips +
Liberation

There are two things you should know about me before we go further. One, I have always had the privilege of being in a body that is deemed socially acceptable, so I can only ever write from that place. Two, I really like potato chips.

I grew up in a very food-neutral household. I ate caldo verde and Sour Keys candy with equal relish. Okay, let's not start with a falsehood. I actually did like vegetables, but candy and potato chips were obviously my darlings. After all, I was a kid.

All my avo (grandmother) cared about was that you were eating. If you were not eating, she would offer you food. If you had just walked through the door, she would offer you food. If you had just finished eating, she would encourage you to finish the leftovers. If there weren't many leftovers, someone must have gone hungry, so she immediately set about making more food.

This worldview made a lot of sense, considering that she grew up on a tiny windswept island in the middle of the Atlantic Ocean at a time when said food was not always in abundance. Food was survival, security, and something to be celebrated. When she arrived in Canada, as long as it was food, it was good. Shake n' Bake, potatoes, and salad existed on equal planes. So that's how I lived too. Looking back, what a gift that was because despite starting out with such a strong foundation, it didn't take long for me to get wrapped up in the usual teenage/wellness stuff of nutritionism and labelling foods as good or bad—and myself as good or bad, depending on which choices I was making.

In my earnest desire to do the best I possibly could for my own health and in wanting to do the same for others, I held a lot of damaging and irrational opinions that now make me cringe. Let's get this straight: the only way the term "clean eating" makes any sense is if you are currently washing your produce. Other memorable moments include allowing myself to think that GMOs were poison while regularly downing a few too many cocktails with my friends and railing against hyper-processed foods as being devoid of nutrition while desperately yearning for chips. In case you thought I was immune to this stuff, I am in fact no stranger to cycles of "being good" followed by cycles of eat-all-the-things.

These restricted foods began to hold such power over me that I couldn't eat a chip without wanting to eat the whole bag. It took a while for me to figure this out, but the only way I could get over it was not to double down on willpower—willpower is a lie—but to let go entirely. I ate all of the chips. So. Many. Chips. Slowly, but surely, those chips started to lose their appeal. Yes, they're still delicious, but I rarely crave them the way that I used to, and sometimes I just straight up don't want them. It turns out the object of my desire was the key to food freedom.

If you're wondering how the heck I could study dietetics while also struggling with my own personal relationship to food, well, humans are not rational beings. If we were, we wouldn't get into half the messes we do now. In fact, the more I learned about the human body and how nutrition interacted with it, the more I was able to let go of the unhelpful mindsets I'd struggled with in the past. And I think that having had this experience makes me better at my job. If I'm making this journey sound easy, it wasn't. Eating is an intimate, deeply held act. I'm also anxious by nature, and learning to trust food and trust my body was actually a long, drawn-out process. If you find yourself in this place, I highly recommend you seek care from a non-diet dietitian or counsellor who can help you untangle your own relationship with food so that it can once again be a source of joy in your life.

As a dietitian, one of the greatest challenges I face in

communicating nutritional information to others is that I know in order to resonate, what I say needs to make sense within your current worldview—even if your worldview isn't grounded in fact. If I come at you with a decade of data about the health benefits of soy foods but you are certain that soy is evil, it probably won't land and instead you'll just tune out. Being able to speak to both your head and your heart at the same time is a key skill, and personal experience gives me a deeper understanding of how we get so tangled up in this stuff in the first place.

Living well is not maintaining a number on a scale or a "free from" diet. And anyone who tells you otherwise isn't interested in your wellbeing. They're interested in their bottom line. It may take time to trust that this is true, but there is no better time than now. When I call out fearmongering on the internet or rail against wellness elitism, it is both from that dietitian place of knowing that the information being shared is inaccurate and from a very personal space of experiencing the harm that such garbage causes firsthand. And you (and I) deserve better.

Soy Curl "Chicken" Fajitas

Serves 4

Gluten-Free Option
Nut-Free
Vegan

My love of soy curls, the dried soybean meat substitute, knows no bounds, and yet somehow this is the first recipe I've created using this versatile ingredient! For my take on this Tex-Mex classic, I am using my favourite technique of roasting to prepare soy curls, inspired by Lauren Toyota of *hot for food*. I find that roasting the soy curls yields a meatier texture and better browning than using the stove top, and by placing everything on a sheet pan, making fajitas got even easier because it's all hands off.

Fajitas

2 cups (500 mL) dry soy curls

2 sweet red peppers, sliced into thin strips

1 medium yellow onion, thinly sliced

1 tablespoon (15 mL) avocado oil

Spice Mixture

1 tablespoon (15 mL) avocado oil

1 tablespoon (15 mL) water

1 tablespoon (15 mL) vegetarian chicken-flavoured stock concentrate

2 teaspoons (10 mL) garlic powder

2 teaspoons (10 mL) chili powder

1 teaspoon (5 mL) onion powder

1 teaspoon (5 mL) ground cumin

1 teaspoon (5 mL) sweet paprika

¼ lime, for squeezing

1. **Soak the soy curls:** In a small bowl, soak the soy curls with enough water to cover by 2 inches (5 cm) for 10 minutes to rehydrate.

2. Meanwhile, preheat the oven to 425°F (220°C). Line a baking sheet with parchment paper.

3. **Make the spice mixture:** In a medium bowl, whisk together the avocado oil, water, stock concentrate, garlic powder, chili powder, onion powder, cumin, sweet paprika, and a squeeze of lime juice.

4. **Coat and roast the soy curls and vegetables:** Drain and squeeze the excess water out of the soy curls. Transfer the soy curls to the bowl of spice mixture. Use your hands to rub the mixture onto the soy curls to coat completely. Spread the coated soy curls on the prepared baking sheet.

5. In the same bowl (no need to wipe; you want to keep any remaining marinade), toss together the sweet peppers, onions, and avocado oil. Scatter the mixture evenly on the baking sheet with the soy curls. Roast until the vegetables have softened and the soy curls are brown and crispy around the edges, 20 to 25 minutes, stirring halfway through.

recipe and ingredients continue

Smashed Avocado

1 ripe avocado, pitted and
    peeled

Juice of ½ lime

Pinch of red chili flakes

Pinch of salt

For serving (optional)

8 (6-inch/15 cm) tortillas,
    warmed

Shredded vegan cheese

Salsa, hot sauce, or Spicy
    Cilantro Garlic Sauce
    (page 293)

Lime wedges

6. **Meanwhile, make the smashed avocado:** In a small bowl, smash the avocado. Mix in the lime juice and a pinch each of chili flakes and salt. Taste and adjust the seasoning as needed.

7. Transfer the roasted soy curls and vegetable mixture to a medium serving bowl. Serve family style with the warmed tortillas, smashed avocado, cheese, and salsa, and lime wedges in separate bowls. Assemble with your favourite fixings.

Swaps + Stuff

For a gluten-free version, use gluten-free stock concentrate and gluten-free tortillas.

Shawarma-Spiced Cauliflower and Chickpea Pita

These Shawarma-inspired pitas are one of my family's favourite meals. Stuffed with addictively spiced roasted cauliflower and chickpeas and drizzled with a spicy tahini sauce, they work well as a meal prep item for lunches all week long. They come together faster than you think: by the time the roasting is done, the sauce and veg will be ready with cleanup time to spare.

Serves 4

Gluten-Free Option
Nut-Free
Vegan

Shawarma-Spiced Cauliflower

1 medium head cauliflower, cut into small florets

1 can (14 ounces/398 mL) chickpeas, rinsed and drained

2 tablespoons (30 mL) avocado oil

2 teaspoons (10 mL) onion powder

1 teaspoon (5 mL) ground cumin

1 teaspoon (5 mL) ground coriander

1 teaspoon (5 mL) fennel seeds

½ teaspoon (2 mL) ground turmeric

½ teaspoon (2 mL) sweet paprika

¼ teaspoon (1 mL) cinnamon

¾ teaspoon (3 mL) salt

Freshly cracked black pepper

1. **Make the shawarma-spiced cauliflower:** Preheat the oven to 425°F (220°C). Line a baking sheet with parchment paper.

2. In a large bowl, toss the cauliflower and chickpeas with the avocado oil, onion powder, cumin, coriander, fennel seeds, turmeric, sweet paprika, cinnamon, salt, and pepper to taste. Spread evenly on the prepared baking sheet and roast until the cauliflower is fork-tender and browned in spots, 25 to 30 minutes, stirring halfway through.

recipe and ingredients continue

Tahini Sauce

⅓ cup (75 mL) tahini

¼ cup (60 mL) freshly squeezed lemon juice

3 tablespoons (45 mL) water

1 clove garlic, grated on a microplane or crushed

½ to 1 jalapeño pepper, seeded and roughly chopped

¼ teaspoon (1 mL) salt

For serving

4 pitas, warmed

1 cup (250 mL) diced English cucumber

1 cup (250 mL) fresh cilantro or parsley leaves and tender stems, finely chopped

¼ cup (60 mL) pitted, chopped Kalamata olives

3. **Meanwhile, make the tahini sauce:** In a small blender, combine the tahini, lemon juice, water, garlic, jalapeño, and salt. Blend until smooth.

4. **Assemble the pitas:** Evenly divide the cauliflower chickpea mixture and pile on the pitas. Drizzle some tahini sauce over top and garnish with cucumber, cilantro, and olives. Store leftover cauliflower chickpea mixture and tahini sauce in separate airtight containers in the fridge for up to 4 days.

Swaps + Stuff

For a gluten-free version, use gluten-free pita or flatbread or swap cooked rice for the pita and serve as a rice bowl.

Roasted Hearts of Palm "Fish" Tacos with Mango Salsa

Is there anything that plants can't do? These "fish" tacos are made with hearts of palm, but I promise you won't miss the fish: hearts of palm is nutrient-dense and has a light and flaky texture that is perfect when paired with fresh mango salsa. These tacos make a light meal on their own or would be delicious served with Kohlrabi Peanut Slaw (page 105) or Herby Potato Salad (page 112) for a heartier meal.

Makes 8 tacos

Gluten-Free Option
Nut-Free
Vegan

Mango Salsa

2 firm ripe mangos, diced

½ cup (125 mL) lightly packed fresh cilantro leaves and tender stems, finely chopped

⅓ cup (75 mL) finely diced red onion

½ jalapeño pepper, diced

Juice of ½ lime

¼ teaspoon (1 mL) salt

Roasted Hearts of Palm "Fish"

1 cup (250 mL) chickpea flour

2 teaspoons (10 mL) onion powder

1¼ teaspoons (6 mL) salt

1½ teaspoons (7 mL) Old Bay seasoning, divided

1 teaspoon (5 mL) ground cumin

Zest of 1 lemon

Freshly cracked black pepper

1 cup (250 mL) water, plus more as needed for thinning

2 cans (14 ounces/398 mL each) whole hearts of palm (see Swaps + Stuff)

2 cups (500 mL) panko crumbs, gluten-free if required

1. **Make the mango salsa:** In a small bowl, toss together the mango, cilantro, red onion, jalapeño, lime juice, and salt. Set aside.

2. **Prepare and bake the hearts of palm:** Preheat the oven to 450°F (230°C). Line a baking sheet with parchment paper.

3. In a medium bowl, stir together the chickpea flour, onion powder, salt, ½ teaspoon (2 mL) of the Old Bay seasoning, cumin, lemon zest, and pepper to taste. Pour in the water and mix until smooth. Let sit for 10 minutes until the mixture thickens to a pourable consistency like pancake batter. If it's too thick, thin with more water, 2 tablespoons (30 mL) at a time, as needed.

4. Meanwhile, cut the hearts of palm in half lengthwise. Gently press the hearts of palm between 2 layers of a kitchen towel or paper towel to remove excess moisture and lightly flatten them.

5. In a small shallow dish, stir together the panko and the remaining 1 teaspoon (5 mL) Old Bay seasoning.

recipe and ingredients continue

For serving

8 small tortillas, warmed

Vegan mayonnaise (optional)

Hot sauce (optional)

Fresh cilantro

Lime wedges

6. Working with one or two hearts of palm pieces at a time, dip the pieces in the chickpea batter to coat. Using a fork, lift each piece out of the batter, allowing excess batter to drip back into the bowl, and dip in the panko mixture to completely coat. Carefully transfer to the prepared baking sheet. Repeat until all the hearts of palm pieces are coated.

7. Bake until golden brown on the bottom, 15 to 20 minutes.

8. **Assemble the tacos:** Spread a bit of mayonnaise, if using, on each tortilla. (I like to make a little spicy mayonnaise with equal parts vegan mayonnaise and hot sauce.) Top with a couple of pieces of roasted hearts of palm, some mango salsa and cilantro. Serve with lime wedges. Store the salsa and roasted hearts of palm in separate airtight containers in the fridge for up to 3 days. Reheat the hearts of palm in a skillet with a drizzle of avocado oil until warmed on both sides.

Swaps + Stuff

For a gluten-free version, use gluten-free tortillas and gluten-free panko crumbs.

If you can't find hearts of palm, canned artichoke hearts work well. During the drying step (see step 4), press firmly between the towels to about ½ inch (1 cm) thickness.

Roasted Broccoli and Butternut Squash Quesadillas

Words to live by: when in doubt, roast it. I think the same could safely be said for making a quesadilla. And these may just be the most delicious quesadillas I've ever made. The roasted vegetable mixture is just a touch sweet and the cashew cream a bit smoky. Up your quesadilla game by taking the time to grill the filled tortillas between two skillets so they get crisp and browned, then lavish them with another drizzle of cashew cream because more is more.

Serves 4

Gluten-Free Option
Nut-Free Option
Vegan

Roasted Vegetable Mixture

1 butternut squash (about 1 pound/450 g), peeled and cut into ½-inch (1 cm) slices

½ pound (225 g) broccoli crowns, cut into small florets

1 medium red onion, cut into 1-inch (2.5 cm) slices

2 tablespoons (30 mL) avocado oil

½ teaspoon (2 mL) ground coriander

½ teaspoon (2 mL) ground cumin

½ teaspoon (2 mL) salt

Freshly cracked black pepper

Paprika Cashew Cream

1¼ cups (300 mL) raw cashews (see Note)

1 cup (250 mL) water

1 clove garlic

1 teaspoon (5 mL) salt

1 teaspoon (5 mL) nutritional yeast

½ teaspoon (2 mL) smoked paprika

½ teaspoon (2 mL) garlic powder

1. **Roast the vegetables:** Preheat the oven to 425°F (220°C). Line a large baking sheet with parchment paper.

2. On the prepared baking sheet, toss the squash, broccoli, and red onions with the avocado oil, coriander, cumin, salt, and pepper to taste. Roast for 20 minutes. Turn the vegetables and continue roasting until the broccoli is golden brown and the squash is soft, another 10 to 15 minutes.

3. **Meanwhile, make the paprika cashew cream:** In a high-speed blender, combine the cashews, water, garlic, salt, nutritional yeast, smoked paprika, and garlic powder. Blend on high speed until smooth, 30 to 60 seconds. Set aside.

4. **Fill and cook the quesadillas:** Spread 2 tablespoons (30 mL) of the paprika cashew cream on a tortilla. Layer a large spoonful of the veggie mixture in the centre of the tortilla, sprinkle with shredded cheese (if using), then fold the tortilla in half to make a half-moon. Repeat with the remaining tortillas.

5. Heat a dry large nonstick skillet over medium heat. Place a filled tortilla in the hot skillet. Use a smaller heavy skillet to press down on the tortilla and cook, turning once until golden brown on each side, 2 to 3 minutes per side.

recipe and ingredients continue

For serving

4 large whole-grain or gluten-free tortillas

Meltable shredded vegan cheese (optional)

6. Drizzle the quesadillas with the remaining paprika cashew cream or serve it on the side as a dipping sauce. The roasted vegetables and cashew cream can be stored in separate airtight containers in the fridge for up to 3 days.

Note: If you don't have a high-speed blender, soak the cashews in water for 4 hours before blending. Drain before using.

Swaps + Stuff

For a gluten-free version, use gluten-free tortillas.

For a nut-free version, swap sunflower seeds, soaked in water overnight and drained, for the cashews. You may need to adjust the flavour with a bit of lemon juice or extra nutritional yeast.

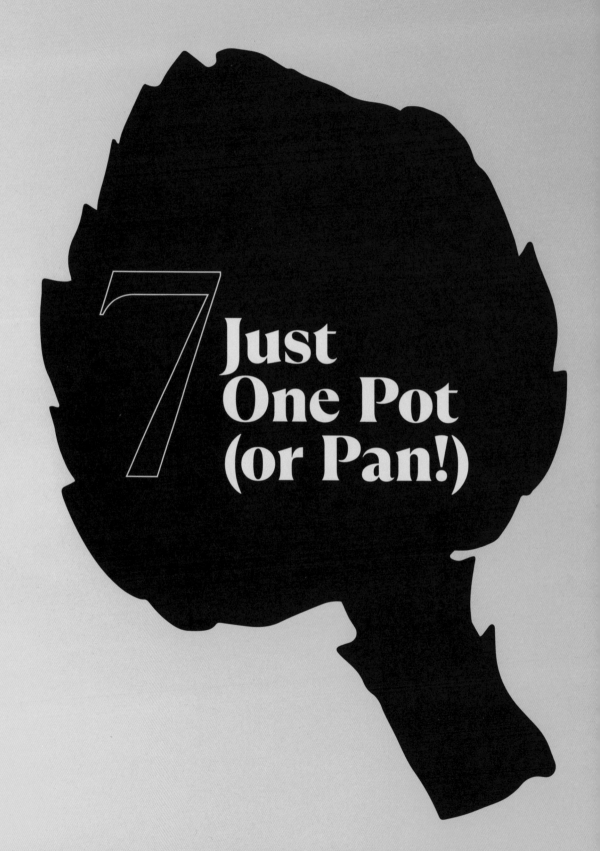

7 Just One Pot (or Pan!)

Greek-Style Gigantes Beans in Tomato Sauce

Serves 6

Gluten-Free Option

Nut-Free

Vegan

When I'm running short on time, I've been known to open a can of gigantes beans in oregano-spiked tomato sauce and eat them straight out of the can. So, it was time I figured out how to make my own. If you have never considered beans craveable, this classic Greek dish is so delicious you might just change your mind. Gigantes beans are large white beans with a creamy yet hearty texture, but they aren't always easy to find. If you can't get your hands on them, substitute butter beans or even cannellini beans. The texture won't quite be the same, but the flavour absolutely will. Cooking times will vary with different beans, and the beans will take longer to cook if they are older.

1 pound (450 g) dried gigantes beans, soaked in water for 12 to 24 hours, drained and rinsed

4 cups (1 L) water

1 can (28 ounces/798 mL) diced tomatoes

1 large yellow onion, finely diced

1 rib celery, finely diced

⅓ cup (75 mL) extra-virgin olive oil

¼ cup (60 mL) packed fresh dill, finely chopped

1 tablespoon (15 mL) chicken-flavoured vegetarian stock concentrate

2 teaspoons (10 mL) cane sugar

2 teaspoons (10 mL) dried oregano

1½ teaspoons (7 mL) salt

Freshly cracked black pepper

Pinch of red chili flakes

Sourdough bread, flatbread, or Black Olive and Za'atar Focaccia (page 224), for serving

1. Preheat the oven to 375°F (190°C).

2. In a Dutch oven or large ovenproof pot, combine the soaked beans, water, tomatoes, onions, celery, olive oil, dill, stock concentrate, sugar, oregano, salt, pepper to taste, and chili flakes. Stir together. Cover with the lid and bake for 2 hours. Remove the lid and bake for another 30 minutes until the beans are soft and the sauce is thick and glistening.

3. Ladle into bowls and enjoy with your favourite bread. Store leftovers in an airtight container in the fridge for up to 5 days.

Swaps + Stuff

For a gluten-free version, use gluten-free stock concentrate. Serve with gluten-free sourdough bread or flatbread.

Spinach and Artichoke One-Pot Pasta

Serves 4

Gluten-Free Option

Nut-Free

Vegan

I cannot tell you how many pounds of spinach and artichoke dip I have consumed in my lifetime, but I assure you it's an impressive amount. I thought it would be fun to create a simple pasta inspired by that classic dip. It's got it all: tons of veg, protein from the beans and pasta (yes, pasta contains protein!), and it comes together in just one pot, no draining required.

1 tablespoon (15 mL) extra-virgin olive or avocado oil

4 cloves garlic, finely chopped

1 package (12 ounces/340 g) whole-grain or gluten-free spaghetti (see Note)

2 cups (500 mL) unsweetened oat milk

2½ cups (625 mL) water

2 teaspoons (10 mL) chicken-flavoured vegetarian stock concentrate

1 can (14 ounces/398 mL) artichoke hearts, drained and chopped

1 can (14 ounces/398 mL) white beans (cannellini or butter), rinsed and drained

3 tablespoons (45 mL) nutritional yeast

2 teaspoons (10 mL) onion powder

1 teaspoon (5 mL) garlic powder

½ teaspoon (2 mL) dried thyme

½ teaspoon (2 mL) salt, plus more for seasoning

6 cups (1.5 L) packed baby spinach

Pinch of red chili flakes

Zest of ½ lemon

¼ cup (60 mL) packed fresh basil leaves, thinly sliced

1. Heat the olive oil in a large pot over medium heat. Add the garlic and cook, stirring for 1 minute.

2. Add the pasta, then pour in the oat milk and water and add the stock concentrate. Increase the heat to high and bring to a boil for 2 full minutes, making sure all the pasta is submerged in the liquid. Reduce the heat to medium-low and add the artichoke hearts, beans, nutritional yeast, onion powder, garlic powder, thyme, and salt and stir. Cover with the lid slightly ajar and cook until the pasta is al dente, about 15 minutes.

3. Remove the lid and stir in the spinach, chili flakes, and lemon zest. Taste and adjust the salt as needed.

4. Divide between bowls and sprinkle with the fresh basil. Store leftovers in an airtight container in the fridge for up to 3 days. Reheat in a saucepan with some water to help revive the sauce and warm over medium heat until steaming.

Note: Using a different pasta shape? I find it takes about double the package cooking time for a true al dente texture (18 minutes for a 9-minute pasta). If the liquid is evaporating too quickly, add more water, ½ cup (125 mL) at a time.

Swaps + Stuff

For a gluten-free version, use gluten-free pasta and gluten-free stock concentrate.

One-Pot Orzo with Spinach and Peas

Serves 4

Gluten-Free Option
Nut-Free
Vegan

Feeding children is not for the faint of heart, and when you find something that works, you stick with it. Pasta with peas has been a kid-friendly dinner hack in my home since my babies were old enough for solids. Consider this a flavourful, family-friendly upgrade that's just as weeknight ready as any of your go-to meals. Orzo, a rice-shaped pasta, is as comforting as it comes, and this one-pot meal is risotto-like in texture and easy to customize to suit picky palettes.

2 tablespoons (30 mL) extra-virgin olive oil

1 large yellow onion, diced

4 cloves garlic, minced

3 cups (750 mL) water

2 cups (500 mL) unsweetened oat milk

2 teaspoons (10 mL) chicken-flavoured vegetarian stock concentrate

2 teaspoons (10 mL) garlic powder

1½ teaspoons (7 mL) dried thyme

1 teaspoon (5 mL) onion powder

1 pound (450 g) dried orzo pasta

6 cups (1.5 L) packed baby spinach, coarsely chopped

1 cup (250 mL) partially thawed frozen peas

3 tablespoons (45 mL) nutritional yeast

2 tablespoons (30 mL) freshly squeezed lemon juice

½ teaspoon (2 mL) salt, plus more for seasoning

¼ cup (60 mL) lightly packed fresh mint leaves, thinly sliced

1. Heat the olive oil in a large pot over medium heat. Add the onions and cook, stirring occasionally, until soft and translucent, 5 to 7 minutes. Add the garlic and stir constantly for 1 minute. Stir in the water, oat milk, stock concentrate, garlic powder, thyme, and onion powder. Bring to a full boil over medium-high heat. Once boiling, stir in the orzo, reduce the heat to medium-low, cover with the lid slightly ajar, and cook, stirring occasionally, until the orzo is al dente and creamy, 10 to 12 minutes.

2. Add the spinach, peas, nutritional yeast, lemon juice, and salt. Cook until the spinach is wilted and the peas are heated through, about 2 minutes. Taste and adjust the salt as needed.

3. Divide between shallow bowls and serve topped with the mint. Store leftovers in an airtight container in the fridge for up to 3 days. Reheat with a few splashes of water in a nonstick skillet to rehydrate the sauce.

Swaps + Stuff

For a gluten-free version, use gluten-free stock concentrate and gluten-free orzo pasta.

Squash and Tomato Curry with Chickpeas

Tomato-based curries don't get nearly as much attention as their coconut milk counterparts here in North America. I humbly offer this chickpea and kabocha curry in hopes of changing your mind. Rich with spices, this nourishing curry is every bit as flavourful and satisfying as the richer coconut milk varieties all on its own as a one-pot meal, or if you'd like to serve a crowd, you can enjoy it with a whole grain like basmati rice or millet. This curry is delicious served with warm naan or chapati.

Serves 4

Gluten-Free Option
Nut-Free
Vegan

- 2 tablespoons (30 mL) avocado or coconut oil
- 1 medium yellow onion, diced
- 1 (2-inch/5 cm) piece fresh ginger, peeled and minced
- 2 teaspoons (10 mL) coriander seeds (or 1 teaspoon/5 mL ground coriander)
- 1 teaspoon (5 mL) cumin seeds (or ½ teaspoon/2 mL ground cumin)
- 1 teaspoon (5 mL) nigella seeds
- 1 teaspoon (5 mL) fennel seeds
- 2 teaspoons (10 mL) curry powder
- 1 teaspoon (5 mL) ground cumin
- ¼ teaspoon (1 mL) cinnamon
- 1 can (28 ounces/798 mL) diced tomatoes
- 1 pound (450 g) kabocha or acorn squash, seeded and cut into 1-inch (2.5 cm) cubes
- 2 cans (14 ounces/398 mL each) chickpeas, rinsed and drained
- 2 cups (500 mL) water
- 2 teaspoons (10 mL) vegetarian stock concentrate
- 1¼ teaspoons (6 mL) salt
- 1 small bunch fresh cilantro leaves and tender stems, finely chopped
- Juice of ½ lime

1. Heat the avocado oil in a large pot over medium heat. Add the onions and cook, stirring occasionally, until soft and translucent, 5 to 7 minutes. Add the ginger, coriander seeds, cumin seeds, nigella seeds, fennel seeds, curry powder, cumin, and cinnamon and cook, stirring constantly, for 1 minute.

2. Add the diced tomatoes, squash, chickpeas, water, stock concentrate, and salt. Stir and bring to a boil over high heat, then reduce the heat to medium, cover with the lid slightly ajar, and cook, stirring occasionally, until the squash is soft, about 20 minutes. Stir in the cilantro and lime juice. Ladle into bowls. Store leftovers in an airtight container in the fridge for up to 4 days or in the freezer for up to 1 month.

Swaps + Stuff

For a gluten-free version, use gluten-free stock concentrate.

Sheet-Pan Gnocchi with Fennel and Kidney Beans

Serves 4 as a light meal

Gluten-Free Option
Nut-Free
Vegan

If you have never roasted gnocchi, you're in for a treat! In the oven, gnocchi take on a hearty chew, so I've gone for a fennel sausage vibe with meaty kidney beans, roasted until split and fluffy. Paired with fennel—a vegetable that doesn't get nearly enough love—red pepper, and onion and drizzled with a roasted garlic dressing. More like a cozy bowl of roasted veggies than a saucy, traditional pasta, this is a one-pan meal that will keep you coming back for more.

Gnocchi with Fennel and Kidney Beans

2 cans (14 ounces/398 mL each) kidney beans, rinsed and drained

2 cups (500 mL) thinly sliced fennel, fronds finely chopped and reserved (1 medium bulb)

1 large sweet red pepper, cut into ½-inch (1 cm) slices

½ large red onion, cut into ½-inch (1 cm) slices

3 tablespoons (45 mL) extra-virgin olive oil, divided

2 teaspoons (10 mL) fennel seeds

1 teaspoon (5 mL) ground cumin

1 teaspoon (5 mL) salt

¼ teaspoon (1 mL) smoked paprika

Freshly cracked black pepper

1 package (1 pound/450 g) gnocchi, gluten-free if required

4 cloves garlic, unpeeled

½ cup (125 mL) fresh flat-leaf parsley leaves and tender stems, finely chopped

1. **Roast the gnocchi with fennel and kidney beans:** Preheat the oven to 425°F (220°C). Line a baking sheet with parchment paper.

2. In a large bowl, toss together the beans, fennel, sweet pepper, and red onions with 2 tablespoons (30 mL) of the olive oil, fennel seeds, cumin, salt, smoked paprika, and black pepper to taste. Spread the mixture evenly on the prepared baking sheet.

3. In the same bowl (no need to wipe), toss the gnocchi with the remaining 1 tablespoon (15 mL) olive oil. Scatter the gnocchi over the vegetables. Nestle in the garlic cloves and roast until the beans are split and the gnocchi is crisp, 30 to 35 minutes. Check the garlic after 25 minutes and remove if it's brown.

recipe and ingredients continue

Dressing

1 tablespoon (15 mL) sherry
    vinegar

2 tablespoons (30 mL) extra-
    virgin olive oil

1 teaspoon (5 mL) cane sugar

Pinch of salt

Freshly cracked black pepper

4. **Meanwhile, make the dressing:** In a small bowl, stir together the sherry vinegar, olive oil, sugar, salt, and pepper to taste.

5. **Finish the dish:** When the gnocchi and vegetables are done, remove from the oven and let sit for a few minutes until the garlic is cool enough to handle.

6. Squeeze the garlic cloves to pop out the roasted garlic. Mix the roasted garlic into the dressing. Drizzle the dressing over the gnocchi and sprinkle with the parsley and reserved fennel fronds. Store leftovers in an airtight container in the fridge for up to 3 days. Reheat with a little olive oil and water to add moisture.

Swaps + Stuff

For a gluten-free version, use gluten-free gnocchi.

Celeriac and White Bean Chili

Serves 4

Gluten-Free Option
Nut-Free
Vegan

2 tablespoons (30 mL) avocado oil

1 medium celeriac, peeled and diced (about 2 heaping cups/600 mL)

1 large yellow onion, diced

3 ribs celery, diced

4 cloves garlic, minced

½ jalapeño pepper, with or without seeds, diced (see Note)

Freshly cracked black pepper

3 cans (14 ounces/398 mL each) white beans (cannellini, navy, or butter), drained and rinsed

1 cup (250 mL) fresh or frozen corn kernels

1 can (4 ounces/125 mL) diced green chilies (see Note)

1 tablespoon (15 mL) dried oregano

2 teaspoons (10 mL) ground cumin

1 teaspoon (5 mL) chili powder

1 teaspoon (5 mL) onion powder

½ teaspoon (2 mL) garlic powder

½ teaspoon (2 mL) salt, plus more for seasoning

4 cups (1 L) water

4 teaspoons (20 mL) chicken-flavoured vegetarian stock concentrate

Everyone needs a good chili (or two!) in their back pocket, and it's the perfect place to experiment with an underappreciated veggie like celeriac. It's got a mild flavour and texture somewhere between a potato and, well, celery! This is my take on a white chili, which has no tomato and uses white beans instead of kidney beans. I've doubled down on heat here, but to keep it kid-friendly, use mild diced green chilies and serve jalapeño on the side for the grownups.

1. Heat the avocado oil in a large pot over medium heat. Add the celeriac, onions, and celery and cook, stirring frequently, until the celeriac begins to soften and brown, 10 to 12 minutes. Toss in the garlic and jalapeño and cook, stirring constantly, for 1 minute. Season with salt and pepper.

2. Add the white beans, corn kernels, green chilies, oregano, cumin, chili powder, onion powder, garlic powder, salt, water, and stock concentrate. Stir and bring to a boil over high heat. Boil for 3 minutes, then reduce the heat to medium and simmer, uncovered, until the celeriac is soft, 15 to 20 minutes.

recipe and ingredients continue

1 cup (250 mL) fresh cilantro
   leaves and tender stems,
   chopped

For serving

1 avocado, peeled, pitted, and
   diced

Lime wedges

3. Using an immersion blender, purée the mixture just a bit (less than a quarter of the mixture) to give the chili a thickened texture. Stir in the cilantro, taste, and adjust the salt and pepper if needed.

4. Ladle into bowls and serve with avocado and lime wedges. Store leftovers in an airtight container in the fridge for up to 4 days or in the freezer for up to 1 month.

Note: This is a moderately spicy chili. To make the chili more child-friendly, seed the jalapeño (or omit entirely) and choose mild diced green chilies.

Swaps + Stuff

For a gluten-free version, use gluten-free stock concentrate.

Dal Palak

Serves 4

Gluten-Free

Nut-Free

Vegan

This simple spinach and red lentil dal is rich with plenty of spices, garlic, and ginger—all three of which are powerful plant medicine. Cumin, coriander, and fennel are all thought to benefit digestion, while turmeric is a potent anti-inflammatory. I've increased the usual amount of water to imagine this as a one-pot meal with a bit of naan or chapati, but you could also serve this as part of a larger meal with basmati rice and Simple and Satisfying Ginger Cabbage (page 82) on the side.

2 tablespoons (30 mL) avocado or coconut oil

1 medium yellow onion, finely diced

3 cloves garlic, chopped

1 (2-inch/5 cm) piece fresh ginger, peeled and chopped

1 teaspoon (5 mL) cumin seeds (or ½ teaspoon/2 mL ground cumin)

1 teaspoon (5 mL) coriander seeds (or ½ teaspoon/2 mL ground coriander)

½ teaspoon (2 mL) ground turmeric

½ teaspoon (2 mL) fennel seeds

⅛ teaspoon (0.5 mL) red chili flakes

4 cups (1 L) water

1 cup (250 mL) dried red lentils

¾ teaspoon (3 mL) salt

4 cups (1 L) packed spinach, chopped

Juice of ½ lime

For serving (optional)

Cooked basmati rice

Naan or chapati, warmed

1. Heat the avocado oil in a large pot over medium heat. Add the onions and cook, stirring occasionally, until very tender and golden, 8 to 12 minutes. If browning too fast, reduce the heat slightly; you want the onions golden, not browned.

2. Add the garlic, ginger, cumin seeds, coriander seeds, turmeric, fennel seeds, and chili flakes and cook, stirring constantly, for 1 minute.

3. Add the water, lentils, and salt and bring to a boil over high heat. Reduce the heat to medium-low, cover with the lid slightly ajar, and cook, stirring occasionally, until the lentils break down and the stew thickens, 15 to 20 minutes.

4. Toss in the spinach and stir until wilted, 1 to 2 minutes. Remove from the heat. Stir in the lime juice. Taste and adjust the salt as needed.

5. Serve with basmati rice, naan, or chapati, if desired. Store leftovers in an airtight container in the fridge for up to 4 days or in the freezer for up to 1 month. Reheat with a splash of water to loosen up the dal.

Baked Mushroom Farotto

Serves 4

Nut-Free

Vegan

This dish is for mushroom lovers. If fungi are the way to your heart like they are to mine, you'll love that dried porcini mushrooms and fresh cremini mushrooms are baked into a dark and brooding farro risotto that is pure decadence. Farro is a varietal of ancient Italian wheat that lends itself to a far heartier and filling dish than traditional risotto all on its own, but if you'd like, some baby arugula dressed simply with a bit of lemon juice and olive oil served on the side will add a vibrant hit of greens.

1 package (½ ounce/14 g) dried porcini mushrooms

1 cup (250 mL) boiling water

2 tablespoons (30 mL) extra-virgin olive oil

1 pound (450 g) cremini mushrooms, halved and sliced

2 shallots, halved and thinly sliced

4 cloves garlic, chopped

Salt and freshly cracked black pepper

1½ cups (375 mL) dried farro

3 cups (750 mL) water

1 tablespoon (15 mL) beef-flavoured vegetarian stock concentrate

3 tablespoons (45 mL) nutritional yeast

1½ teaspoons (7 mL) garlic powder

1½ teaspoons (7 mL) dried thyme

2 tablespoons (30 mL) tomato paste

2 tablespoons (30 mL) vegan butter

Squeeze of lemon juice

¼ cup (60 mL) packed fresh curly parsley or dill, minced, for serving (optional)

1. Preheat the oven to 350°F (180°C).

2. Place the dried porcini mushrooms in a small bowl and cover with the boiling water. Let sit for 10 minutes to rehydrate. Remove the mushrooms from the water and carefully squeeze out excess liquid back into the bowl. Reserve the soaking liquid. Roughly chop the mushrooms.

3. Heat the olive oil in a large heavy-bottomed pot or Dutch oven over medium-high heat. Reduce the heat to medium, add the cremini mushrooms and shallots, and cook, stirring occasionally, until the mushrooms are browned and water has released, 7 to 9 minutes. Add the garlic and cook, stirring constantly, for 1 minute. Season to taste with salt and pepper.

4. Add the farro, porcini mushrooms, and reserved soaking liquid. Cook, stirring constantly, scraping any brown bits from the bottom of the pan, until the liquid is mostly absorbed, 2 to 3 minutes. Stir in the water, stock concentrate, nutritional yeast, garlic powder, thyme, and tomato paste. Cover with a lid, transfer to the oven, and bake until the farro is thick and creamy like risotto, 30 to 40 minutes.

5. Finish by stirring in the butter and a squeeze of lemon juice. Taste and adjust the seasoning as needed. (I add about ¼ teaspoon/1 mL salt.) Divide among shallow bowls and sprinkle with the parsley or dill, if using. Store leftovers in an airtight container in the fridge for up to 3 days or in the freezer for up to 1 month.

Shiitake and Smoked Tofu Fried Rice

Serves 2 to 3

Gluten-Free
Low-FODMAP Option
Nut-Free
Vegan

Growing up in a small town, every birthday meant a special dinner from Polly's Café, our town's Chinese-Canadian restaurant. My love of fried rice started there, but the origins of this dish can be traced back thousands of years to Yangzhou, China. I've loaded my version with plenty of vegetables and tofu but kept the seasoning light so as not to overshadow the rice itself. This dish comes together quickly, so ensure that you have all the ingredients ready to go before you start cooking.

1 tablespoon (15 mL) sesame oil

1 tablespoon (15 mL) gluten-free tamari

1 tablespoon (15 mL) chili bean paste or gluten-free chili garlic hot sauce

2 tablespoons (30 mL) avocado or refined coconut oil, divided

½ pound (225 g) shiitake mushrooms, sliced and long stems chopped

1 package (6 ounces/170 g) smoked tofu or tempeh, diced

1 tablespoon (15 mL) minced peeled fresh ginger

2 cloves garlic, chopped

½ pound (225 g) snap peas, cut diagonally into ½-inch (1 cm) pieces (or 1 cup/250 mL frozen peas)

4 cups (1 L) packed baby spinach

1 small bunch green onions, thinly sliced

Salt and white pepper

3 cups (750 mL) cooked long-grain brown rice

1. In a small bowl, stir together the sesame oil, tamari, and chili bean paste. Set aside.

2. Heat 1 tablespoon (15 mL) of the avocado oil in a large nonstick skillet over medium-high heat. Toss in the mushrooms and cook, stirring occasionally, until golden, 5 to 7 minutes. Reduce the heat to medium, add the tofu, ginger, and garlic, and cook, stirring constantly, for 1 minute.

3. Add the snap peas, spinach, and green onions and cook, stirring frequently, until the spinach wilts and the snap peas look glossy, 2 to 3 minutes. Season to taste with salt and white pepper. Transfer the vegetable mixture to a medium bowl.

4. In the same pan (no need to wipe) over medium heat, add the remaining 1 tablespoon (15 mL) avocado oil and rice and cook, stirring frequently, until warmed through, 1 to 2 minutes. Turn off the heat and leave the skillet on the element. Season to taste with salt. Return the veggies to the skillet along with the sesame oil mixture and stir through. Divide between bowls and serve. Store leftovers in an airtight container in the fridge for up to 3 days.

Swaps + Stuff

For a low-FODMAP version, omit the snap peas and garlic. Use garlic-free hot sauce and only the dark green part of the green onions. Swap oyster mushrooms for the shiitake mushrooms.

Lemony Chickpea and Potato Stew

Serves 4

Gluten-Free Option

Nut-Free

Vegan

This bright and sunny stew is inspired by a dish I ate at Delara, an incredible Persian restaurant in Vancouver. It's flavoured with preserved lemon, which lends a complex, citrusy note that's tangy and savoury at the same time. Best of all, my Simple Preserved Lemons (page 296) are very easy to make, although they do take some time, so I've offered a variation in case you find yourself with a craving but without preserved lemons on hand (see Swaps + Stuff).

2 tablespoons (30 mL) extra-virgin olive oil

1 medium yellow onion, finely diced

4 cloves garlic, chopped

4 cups (1 L) water

2 cans (14 ounces/398 mL each) chickpeas, rinsed and drained

1 pound (450 g) baby potatoes, cut into bite-size pieces

1 tablespoon (15 mL) chicken-flavoured vegetarian stock concentrate

¾ teaspoon (3 mL) salt, plus more for seasoning

1 teaspoon (5 mL) dried oregano

1 teaspoon (5 mL) ground turmeric

1 fresh or dried bay leaf

Juice of 1 lemon (3 to 4 tablespoons/45 to 60 mL)

Peel from ½ Simple Preserved Lemon (page 296), rinsed and diced

¼ cup (60 mL) tahini

2 cups (500 mL) lightly packed greens (Swiss chard, collard greens, kale), finely chopped (optional)

Freshly cracked black pepper

1. Heat the olive oil in a large pot over medium heat. Add the onions and cook, stirring occasionally, until soft and translucent, 5 to 7 minutes.

2. Add the garlic and cook, stirring constantly, for 1 minute. Stir in the water, chickpeas, potatoes, stock concentrate, salt, oregano, turmeric, and bay leaf. Bring to a boil over high heat for 5 minutes, then reduce the heat to medium, add the lemon juice and diced preserved lemon peel (or fresh lemon peel, salt, and cumin mixture), and cook, uncovered, for another 15 minutes until the potatoes are fork-tender. Remove from the heat.

3. Place the tahini in a small bowl. Add a few tablespoons of the broth and mix well until smooth. Stir the tahini mixture into the broth. Add the greens (if using) and stir. If using fresh lemon peel, remove it along with the bay leaf and discard. Taste and adjust the salt and pepper if needed. Store leftovers in an airtight container in the fridge for up to 3 days or in the freezer for up to 1 month.

Swaps + Stuff

For a gluten-free version, use gluten-free stock concentrate.

If you don't have Simple Preserved Lemons on hand, you can use the peel from 1 fresh lemon. Cut the peel into four (2-inch/5 cm) strips. Combine the lemon strips with ¼ teaspoon (1 mL) salt, and ¼ teaspoon (1 mL) ground cumin. Mix.

Sheet-Pan Paprika and Brown Sugar Tofu

Saucy, savoury, and just a touch sweet, this sheet pan meal takes less than 15 minutes of hands-on time so you can get on with it. Don't let the longer ingredient list deter you, it's mostly spices that you probably already have in your pantry! The cherry tomatoes burst as they roast, so there is no need for an additional sauce. This dish is a comforting and well-balanced meal, with greens, potatoes, and protein-rich tofu.

Serves 4

Gluten-Free
Low-FODMAP Option
Nut-Free
Vegan

3 tablespoons (45 mL) brown sugar

3 tablespoons (45 mL) avocado oil, divided

1 tablespoon (15 mL) apple cider vinegar

1 teaspoon (5 mL) sweet paprika

1 teaspoon (5 mL) onion powder

1 teaspoon (5 mL) ground cumin

1 teaspoon (5 mL) salt

½ teaspoon (2 mL) smoked paprika

½ teaspoon (2 mL) dried oregano

¼ teaspoon (1 mL) red chili flakes or cayenne pepper

1 package (12 ounces/340 g) extra-firm tofu, cut into ¾-inch (2 cm) cubes

1½ pounds (675 g) baby potatoes, halved

1 pint (2 cups/500 mL) cherry tomatoes, halved

4 cups (1 L) lightly packed baby arugula

1. Preheat the oven to 425°F (220°C). Line a baking sheet with parchment paper.

2. In a large bowl, mix together the brown sugar, 1 tablespoon (15 mL) of the avocado oil, apple cider vinegar, sweet paprika, onion powder, cumin, salt, smoked paprika, oregano, and chili flakes into a paste.

3. Toss the tofu in the marinade. Use your hands to rub the marinade onto the tofu to ensure it is coated all over. Place the tofu on one side of the prepared baking sheet.

4. In the same bowl (no need to wipe), drizzle in the remaining 2 tablespoons (30 mL) avocado oil. Add the potatoes and tomatoes and toss until well coated.

5. Spread the potatoes and tomatoes on the other side of the prepared baking sheet in an even layer. Roast until the potatoes are fork-tender and the tofu is golden brown, 40 to 45 minutes, stirring halfway through. Remove from the oven. Top with the arugula and toss to combine before serving. Store leftovers in an airtight container in the fridge for up to 3 days.

Swaps + Stuff

For a low-FODMAP version, swap chopped Roma tomatoes for the cherry tomatoes and omit the onion powder. You may wish to swap garlic-flavoured oil for the avocado oil to add more flavour.

8 Things for Sharing + Snacking

Sumac and Date Party Mix

**Makes 5 cups (1.25 L),
serves 10**

Gluten-Free Option
Nut-Free Option
Vegan

⅓ cup (75 mL) extra-virgin olive
   oil

1 tablespoon (15 mL) ground
   sumac

1 tablespoon (15 mL) cane sugar

1¼ teaspoons (6 mL) salt

1 teaspoon (5 mL) dried thyme

½ teaspoon (2 mL) garlic powder

Pinch of red chili flakes

1 cup (250 mL) raw almonds

1 cup (250 mL) raw cashews

3 cups (750 mL) puffed wheat or
   Kamut cereal

½ cup (125 mL) pitted Medjool
   dates, sliced

I'm here for the party and I've brought snacks. Inspired by my mother-in-law, Wendy—who makes a mean bits and bites party mix—I figured it was probably time for me to create my own party mix for family gatherings. And, of course, it was going to skew Eastern Mediterranean with citrusy sumac and dates, but I couldn't resist a retro leaning with puffed wheat cereal. You're going to want to eat this all the time. It doesn't last long!

1. Preheat the oven to 325°F (160°C). Line a baking sheet with parchment paper.

2. In a large bowl, whisk together the olive oil, sumac, sugar, salt, thyme, garlic powder, and chili flakes. Toss in the almonds and cashews to evenly coat. Add the puffed wheat and dates and toss again.

3. Scrape the mixture onto the prepared baking sheet and spread into an even layer. Bake until the nuts and cereal look golden and most of the moisture is absorbed, 15 to 18 minutes, stirring halfway through. Remove from the oven, transfer the pan to a rack, and let the mixture cool completely before serving. Store in an airtight container on the counter for up to 1 week.

Swaps + Stuff

For a gluten-free version, swap rice squares cereal for the puffed wheat or Kamut cereal.

For a nut-free version, swap 2 cups (500 mL) of your favourite raw seeds for the almonds and cashews.

Coriander Chili Hummus Bowl

Serves 4

Gluten-Free

Nut-Free

Vegan

I am quite low key when it comes to having friends over for a meal. One of my signature appetizers is a hummus bowl, where I pile a bunch of herbs, olives, or jarred vegetables on a bed of creamy hummus. Even when you make your own hummus, this crowd-pleaser takes just 15 minutes to make, and it's usually the first to go on the snack table. It's a great dip for fresh sliced vegetables, pita, or crackers.

Hummus

1 can (14 ounces/398 mL) chickpeas, rinsed and drained

¼ cup (60 mL) tahini

¼ cup (60 mL) freshly squeezed lemon juice

2 tablespoons (30 mL) extra-virgin olive oil

1 clove garlic, crushed or grated on a microplane

¾ teaspoon (3 mL) salt

3 tablespoons (45 mL) ice water

⅓ cup (75 mL) lightly packed fresh cilantro leaves and tender stems, minced

½ teaspoon (2 mL) ground coriander

⅛ teaspoon (0.5 mL) ground cumin

½ small fresh red chili, sliced (or ¼ teaspoon/1 mL red chili flakes)

Garnishes (optional)

Diced jarred roasted red peppers

Chopped pitted Kalamata or Castelvetrano olives

Fresh cilantro or curly parsley leaves and tender stems, minced

Extra-virgin olive oil

Ground sumac or Simple Za'atar (page 292) or store-bought

Flaky sea salt

1. In a small food processor, combine the chickpeas, tahini, lemon juice, olive oil, garlic, and salt. Blend until thick. With the processor running, add the water and blend for 2 minutes until smooth and creamy, stopping once to scrape down the sides of the bowl. Taste and adjust the salt if needed. Add the cilantro, coriander, cumin, and chili. Pulse a few times to combine.

2. Scrape the hummus into a medium serving bowl. Garnish with roasted red peppers, olives, cilantro or parsley, and drizzle with olive oil. Sprinkle with sumac or za'atar and flaky sea salt, if desired. (Feel free to garnish with whatever vegetables, herbs, or seasoning you have on hand.) Store leftover hummus, with the garnishes, in an airtight container in the fridge for up to 5 days.

Note: The flavour of chickpeas and tahini vary, and any bitterness will affect the flavour of the hummus. The fix? Try adding a bit of maple syrup, ½ teaspoon (2 mL) at a time, as sugar offsets bitterness. Taste after each addition, as you don't want the hummus to be sweet.

Black Olive and Za'atar Focaccia

Makes 1 (9 × 13-inch/ 23 × 32 cm) slab

Nut-Free

Vegan

Baking bread does not come naturally to me; in fact, most of my previous recipe experiments have been by necessity, wanting to create nutrient-dense alternatives for my gut health clients. But then I took a cooking class online with the wonderful Alexandra Stafford, during which I made focaccia for the first time, and I was hooked! There is no more decadent bread: with Alexandra's method as a guide, this easy-to-make, pillowy bread is lavished with olive oil and studded with olives, za'atar, and plenty of flaky sea salt. Pure pleasure.

2 cups (500 mL) warm water

1 tablespoon (15 mL) active dry yeast

1 teaspoon (5 mL) cane sugar

3 cups (750 mL) all-purpose flour

1 cup (250 mL) whole wheat or whole-grain spelt flour

2 teaspoons (10 mL) salt

5 tablespoons (75 mL) extra-virgin olive oil, divided, plus more for your hands

Cold vegan butter, for greasing the baking dish

1 tablespoon (15 mL) Simple Za'atar (page 292) or store-bought

2 teaspoons (10 mL) flaky sea salt

¼ cup (60 mL) pitted Kalamata olives, halved

1. Pour the warm water into a medium bowl. Stir in the yeast and sugar. Let sit for 5 minutes to activate the yeast. It should look cloudy or foamy; if not, the yeast is too old and you should start again with fresh yeast.

2. In a large bowl, stir together the all-purpose flour, whole wheat flour, and salt. Pour the flour mixture into the bowl of water. Using a wooden spoon, mix together until a wet, shaggy dough forms with no dry patches. Remove the dough from the bowl.

3. Wipe the empty large bowl clean. Brush the bowl with 1 tablespoon (15 mL) of the olive oil. Place the dough in the bowl. Drizzle 1 tablespoon (15 mL) of the olive oil on top of the dough and smear it over the dough with your hands. Cover the bowl with plastic wrap and allow the dough to rise in a warm, draft-free place until it has doubled in size, about 2 hours. (You can also let the dough rise inside a cold oven with the light on and the door closed.)

4. Preheat the oven to 425°F (220°C). Grease a 13 × 9-inch (3.5 L) glass baking dish thoroughly with cold butter. Then brush the dish with 1 tablespoon (15 mL) of the olive oil.

5. Once the dough has doubled in size, uncover the bowl, deflate the dough by pulling it toward the centre of the bowl with a fork, and tip it into the prepared baking dish. Cover with plastic wrap and allow the dough to rise in a warm, draft-free place for 30 minutes. The dough should rise to almost fill the dish.

6. With lightly oiled hands, use your fingers to press deep holes into the dough. Drizzle the dough with the remaining 2 tablespoons (30 mL) olive oil. Sprinkle with za'atar and flaky sea salt, and top with the olives. Bake until the top and bottom look crisp and golden brown, 25 to 30 minutes. Remove the focaccia from the oven and allow it to cool in the dish for 15 minutes. Carefully remove the bread from the pan and enjoy warm or transfer it to a rack to cool completely. Store the focaccia, loosely covered, on the counter for up to 3 days.

Tempeh Nachos

Serves 4

Gluten-Free Option

Nut-Free

Vegan

Nachos are a love language, and I promise that these will have you hooked on tempeh, tofu's fermented Indonesian cousin. Tempeh has a nutty, earthy flavour that can be intimidating for novice cooks, but when simmered in a richly flavoured sauce it is sure to wow. I've added some sneaky veggies in the sauce, so you don't need a lot of additional toppings. The simmered tempeh also makes a great filling for burritos or a meal prep addition to grain bowls.

1 tablespoon (15 mL) avocado or extra-virgin olive oil

1 medium yellow onion, finely diced

1 sweet red pepper, diced

1 package (6 ounces/170 g) tempeh, crumbled

2 cloves garlic, minced

1 cup (250 mL) water

2 tablespoons (30 mL) tomato paste

1 tablespoon (15 mL) beef-flavoured vegetarian stock concentrate

2 teaspoons (10 mL) chili powder

2 teaspoons (10 mL) dried oregano

1 teaspoon (5 mL) ground cumin

1 teaspoon (5 mL) sweet paprika

1 bag (12 ounces/340 g) tortilla chips

3 cups (750 mL) meltable vegan cheese shreds

½ jalapeño pepper, thinly sliced (optional)

½ cup (125 mL) finely chopped fresh cilantro leaves and tender stems

1. Line a large baking sheet with parchment paper.

2. Heat the avocado oil in a large nonstick skillet over medium heat. Add the onions and sweet pepper and cook, stirring occasionally, until the vegetables start to soften, 2 to 3 minutes. Add the tempeh and cook, stirring frequently, until well browned, 5 to 7 minutes. Add the garlic and cook, stirring constantly, for 1 minute.

3. Pour in the water and add the tomato paste and stock concentrate. Stir to combine. Add the chili powder, oregano, cumin, and sweet paprika. Bring the mixture to a boil, then reduce the heat to medium-low and simmer, uncovered, until the liquid is mostly absorbed but the mixture looks a bit saucy, not dry, 4 to 5 minutes. Taste and adjust with salt if needed. Remove from the heat.

4. Meanwhile, place a rack in the upper third of the oven and preheat the broiler to high.

5. Spread the tortilla chips evenly on the prepared baking sheet. Layer the tempeh mixture over the chips and top with the cheese. Broil until the cheese is bubbly, watching carefully so it doesn't burn. Sprinkle with jalapeños (if using) and cilantro and serve. Store leftovers in an airtight container in the fridge for up to 3 days. To reheat, bake in a 400°F (200°C) oven until warmed through.

Swaps + Stuff

For a gluten-free version, use gluten-free stock concentrate.

Roasted Eggplant Dip with **Sundried Tomatoes** and **Walnuts**

If we're ever at a party together, you'll know where to find me: scoping out the dip situation. I've never met a dip I didn't like, and transforming vegetables into a more scoopable form is one of my favourite things. Roasted eggplant creates a silky base for sundried tomatoes and walnuts to do their umami thing with just a touch of fennel to have people asking, "What is that deliciousness?" This is a small batch, so be sure to double it for a party!

Makes about 1¼ cups (300 mL)

Gluten-Free

Vegan

1 medium Italian eggplant (about 1 pound/450 g)

¼ cup (60 mL) avocado oil, divided

¾ teaspoon (3 mL) salt, divided

½ teaspoon (2 mL) ground cumin

Freshly cracked black pepper

4 unpeeled cloves garlic

⅓ cup (75 mL) jarred sundried tomatoes packed in oil, patted dry (see Note)

½ cup (125 mL) raw walnuts

1 tablespoon (15 mL) freshly squeezed lemon juice

1 teaspoon (5 mL) nutritional yeast

¼ teaspoon (1 mL) fennel seeds

1. Preheat the oven to 425°F (220°C). Line a baking sheet with parchment paper.

2. Cut the eggplant into 1-inch (2.5 cm) cubes. Scatter the eggplant on the prepared baking sheet. Drizzle 2 tablespoons (30 mL) of the avocado oil over top. Sprinkle with ½ teaspoon (2 mL) of the salt, cumin, and lots of pepper. Toss to coat. Nestle the unpeeled garlic in the middle of the baking sheet. Roast the eggplant until golden brown on the bottom, about 30 minutes. Do not stir. Check the garlic after 20 minutes and remove if needed to avoid browning.

3. Remove from the oven and let the eggplant mixture cool on the baking sheet for 10 minutes. Once the garlic is cool enough to handle, peel off the skin and discard.

recipe continues

4. In a small food processor, combine the sundried tomatoes and walnuts. Pulse until finely chopped. Add the eggplant, peeled garlic, lemon juice, nutritional yeast, the remaining ¼ teaspoon (1 mL) salt, fennel seeds, and more pepper. Blend until mostly smooth with some eggplant peel visible. Stir in the remaining 2 tablespoons (30 mL) avocado oil by hand. If you prefer a light, more whipped texture, stir in 2 to 4 tablespoons (30 to 60 mL) water. Taste and adjust the salt, pepper, and lemon juice if needed. Store leftovers in an airtight container in the fridge for up to 3 days. It will thicken in the fridge. Adjust to desired texture with water, 1 tablespoon (15 mL) at a time.

Note: Be sure to add the avocado oil and water (if using) as the last step as instructed, otherwise the fibre in the eggplant will soak them up too quickly and the dip will have a firm texture. If the eggplant thickens too much, loosen with a bit of water.

If using dry sundried tomatoes, soak them in hot water for 10 minutes, then pat dry and continue with the recipe.

Carrot and Za'atar Pancakes with Spicy Cilantro Garlic Sauce

I am of the mind that za'atar makes anything more delicious, and I think these carrot pancakes will make you a believer too. Somewhere between a latke and socca, there are so many ways to use these sunny little pancakes! Great as an appetizer or addition to a snack board, you can also use them as a veggie burger alternative or enjoy two or three as a side dish. Don't skip the cilantro garlic sauce; in fact, you may wish to make a double batch.

Makes 15 pancakes, serves 4 to 6

Gluten-Free

Nut-Free

Vegan

1½ cups (375 mL) chickpea flour

2 tablespoons (30 mL) ground flaxseed

2 teaspoons (10 mL) Simple Za'atar (page 292) or store-bought

1½ teaspoons (7 mL) salt

1 clove garlic, grated on a microplane

½ teaspoon (2 mL) ground cumin

½ teaspoon (2 mL) garlic powder

½ teaspoon (2 mL) ground turmeric

Freshly cracked black pepper

1 cup (250 mL) lukewarm water

1 pound (450 g) carrots, well scrubbed and grated

4 green onions, thinly sliced

Avocado or coconut oil, for frying

Spicy Cilantro Garlic Sauce (page 293), for serving

1. Preheat the oven to 200°F (100°C). Line a baking sheet with parchment paper.

2. In a medium bowl, stir together the chickpea flour, flax-seed, za'atar, salt, garlic, cumin, garlic powder, turmeric, and pepper to taste. Pour in the water and mix until no lumps remain. Let sit for 10 minutes to thicken.

3. Stir in the carrots and green onions. The mixture should look like a pourable thick pancake batter. If the batter is too thick, add more water, 2 tablespoons (30 mL) at a time, until the correct consistency is reached.

recipe continues

4. Heat 1 tablespoon (15 mL) of the avocado oil in a large nonstick skillet over medium heat. Cooking in batches, scoop ¼ cup (60 mL) of batter per pancake into the pan. Using the back of the scoop, flatten the batter a bit and cook until golden brown on the bottom, 2 to 4 minutes. Carefully flip, gently flatten the pancake, and cook for another 2 to 4 minutes. (If the pancakes are sticking to the pan, they're not ready to flip.) Reduce the heat to medium-low if the pancakes are browning too fast; you want the vegetables to cook through. Transfer the pancakes to the prepared baking sheet and keep warm in the oven. Repeat to use the remaining batter, adding more avocado oil to the pan as needed.

5. Serve the pancakes with spicy cilantro garlic sauce. The sauce and pancakes can be stored in separate airtight containers in the fridge for up to 3 days. The pancakes can also be stored in the freezer for up to 1 month. To reheat, pop the pancakes in the toaster until warmed through.

Herby Date Bites

Makes 12 bites

Gluten-Free

Vegan

12 Medjool dates, pitted

¼ cup (60 mL) Herbed Cashew Cheese (page 297) or store-bought semi-firm cashew cheese

12 raw almonds, chopped

Flaky sea salt

Red chili flakes

File this one under snacks that look fancy but are super easy to make. It will also help you use up any cashew cheese you have left in the fridge. Sweet, salty, and flecked with spicy red chili flakes, this is the perfect snack to whip up when friends pop by or you've just got a craving.

1. Slice the dates in half lengthwise, taking care not to cut all the way through, and open them to form a pocket. Stuff each date with 1 teaspoon (5 mL) of the herbed cashew cheese and top with a sprinkle of chopped almonds.

2. Arrange the stuffed dates on a serving plate. Sprinkle with the flaky sea salt and chili flakes. Store leftovers in an air-tight container in the fridge for up to 1 day.

Herbed Seed Pâté

**Makes about 2 cups
(500 mL)**

Gluten-Free

Nut-Free

Vegan

It's time for a modern take on pâté with nutrient-dense seeds claiming the culinary spotlight. I love finding new ways to cook with seeds, because they are packed with minerals and protein—we really don't eat them as often as we should. This is a rich spread, so a little goes a long way! This recipe will serve a crowd and makes a great little hostess gift, but feel free to prepare a half-batch if making to have on hand for snacks.

1 cup (250 mL) raw pumpkin seeds, soaked in water for at least 4 hours or overnight and drained

1 cup (250 mL) hemp hearts

¼ cup (60 mL) extra-virgin olive oil

¼ cup (60 mL) water

¼ cup (60 mL) freshly squeezed lemon juice

¼ cup (60 mL) sundried tomatoes packed in oil, patted dry

1 clove garlic

1 teaspoon (5 mL) ground coriander

½ teaspoon (2 mL) onion powder

1 teaspoon (5 mL) salt

½ cup (125 mL) packed fresh basil leaves

½ cup (125 mL) lightly packed flat-leaf parsley leaves and tender stems

For serving

Gluten-free or whole-grain crackers

1. In a food processor, combine the drained pumpkin seeds, hemp hearts, olive oil, water, lemon juice, sundried tomatoes, garlic, coriander, onion powder, and salt. Blend until thick and smooth, 3 to 4 minutes. If the mixture is too thick to be easily spreadable, add more water, 1 tablespoon (15 mL) at a time. Don't add too much water; the mixture should be thick and spreadable.

2. Add the basil and parsley and blend for 1 minute to incorporate. Serve with gluten-free or whole-grain crackers. Store leftovers in an airtight container in the fridge for up to 5 days.

Sweet Potato Harissa Dip

Makes about 1½ cups (375 mL)

Gluten-Free

Nut-Free

Vegan

This dip features two of my favourite things—creamy tahini and spicy harissa—teaming up to transform sweet potatoes into a craveable dip that is right at home on a snack board, a grain bowl, or a sandwich. If you have leftover roasted sweet potatoes, this dip whips up in just a few minutes! It's everything you love about sweet potatoes, just in dip form.

1 pound (450 g) sweet potatoes, scrubbed and cut into 1-inch (2.5 cm) cubes

1 tablespoon (15 mL) avocado oil

⅓ cup (75 mL) tahini

1 tablespoon (15 mL) harissa paste, plus more to taste

1 teaspoon (5 mL) ground cumin

1 teaspoon (5 mL) onion powder

1 tablespoon (15 mL) pure maple syrup

1 tablespoon (15 mL) freshly squeezed lemon juice

2 tablespoons (30 mL) water

½ teaspoon (2 mL) salt, plus more for seasoning

⅓ cup (75 mL) fresh curly parsley leaves and tender stems, minced

For serving (optional)

Sliced vegetables

Tortilla chips

Whole-grain crackers

1. Preheat the oven to 425°F (220°C). Line a baking sheet with parchment paper.

2. Scatter the sweet potatoes on the prepared baking sheet. Toss with the avocado oil and some salt. Roast until fork-tender, 30 to 40 minutes, stirring halfway through. Remove from the oven and let the potatoes cool on the baking sheet for 5 minutes.

3. In a food processor, combine the roasted sweet potato, tahini, harissa, cumin, onion powder, maple syrup, lemon juice, water, and salt. Blend until smooth. Taste and adjust the salt or harissa for more heat, if needed. Transfer the dip to a serving bowl and swirl in the parsley. Serve with sliced vegetables, tortilla chips, or whole-grain crackers, if desired. Store leftover dip in an airtight container in the fridge for up to 4 days.

Spicy Tofu Nuggets

Serves 4 as a snack

Gluten-Free

Nut-Free

Vegan

It's always hard to pick favourites, but if there is one recipe in this book that has effortlessly worked its way into our weekly rotation, it's these fiery tofu nuggets. Inspired by Buffalo *everything,* the tofu is torn instead of cut, creating lots of nooks and crannies for the garlicky hot sauce to cling to. Enjoy as a snack with Cashew Tzatziki (page 295) or Tahini Ranch (page 111) or as a protein boost in your favourite grain bowl or burrito. Alternatively, you can slice the tofu block crosswise into four equal pieces and prepare the recipe as a sandwich filler. This spicy tofu is so versatile, you might want to get in the habit of making a double batch!

1 package (12 ounces/340 g) extra-firm tofu, patted dry

3 tablespoons (45 mL) Buffalo-style hot sauce

1 tablespoon (15 mL) avocado oil

1 teaspoon (5 mL) garlic powder

1 teaspoon (5 mL) onion powder

½ teaspoon (2 mL) salt

¼ teaspoon (1 mL) cayenne pepper

2 tablespoons (30 mL) cornstarch

1 green onion, dark part only, thinly sliced, for garnish

Cashew Tzatziki (page 295) or Tahini Ranch (page 111), for serving

1. Preheat the oven to 400°F (200°C). Line a small baking sheet with parchment paper.

2. Tear the tofu in half horizontally, then tear the halves into 1-inch (2.5 cm) pieces.

3. In a medium bowl, whisk together the hot sauce, avocado oil, garlic powder, onion powder, salt, and cayenne pepper. Toss the tofu in the sauce mixture. Sprinkle the cornstarch over top and toss well to coat. Spread the tofu evenly on the prepared baking sheet. Bake for 20 minutes. Flip and bake for another 10 minutes until the edges are golden brown.

4. Transfer the spicy tofu nuggets to a serving plate. Garnish with the green onions. Serve with your favourite sauce on the side for dipping. Store leftovers in an airtight container in the fridge for up to 4 days.

9 Really Good Sweets

Creamy Lemon Ginger Ice Pops

Lemon and ginger go together like peanut butter and jam—whether in my Sniffle Soother tonic (page 288) or in these simple ice pops. Ginger is one of those plant medicines that I try to work into my diet daily if I can, and I love the zing it adds to these yummy, refreshing treats.

Makes 6 ice pops

Gluten-Free
Low-FODMAP
Nut-Free
Vegan

1 can (14 ounces/398 mL) full-fat coconut milk

3 tablespoons (45 mL) pure maple syrup

1 (2-inch/5 cm) piece fresh ginger, peeled

Zest of 1 lemon

¼ cup (60 mL) freshly squeezed lemon juice

1. In a high-speed blender, combine the coconut milk, maple syrup, ginger, and lemon zest. Blend on high speed for 30 seconds until smooth. Add the lemon juice and blend on low speed for 10 seconds to incorporate.

2. Pour the mixture into 6 ice-pop moulds and freeze for at least 12 hours until firm. The ice pops can be stored in the freezer for up to 1 month.

3. To remove the ice pops from the moulds, gently squeeze the pop as you pull the handle. If it does not release, run the mould under warm water for a few seconds and try again.

Thin Mint Cookies

Makes 18 cookies

Gluten-Free

Vegan

Given how much I love the pairing of chocolate and mint, without a doubt, thin mints are a top-five cookie for me. And this recipe is easily the best thin mint I have ever had. The wafer leans ever so slightly toward bittersweet, so it balances the chocolatey coating perfectly. And for my troubled tummy buddies, here's a hack: swap the peppermint flavour in the coating to ½ teaspoon (2 mL) pure culinary peppermint oil for a tummy-soothing treat.

Cookies

⅓ cup (75 mL) coconut oil

⅓ cup (75 mL) unsweetened almond milk

1¼ cups (300 mL) almond flour

¼ cup (60 mL) arrowroot powder

½ teaspoon (2 mL) salt

¼ teaspoon (1 mL) baking powder

1 cup (250 mL) cocoa powder

⅓ cup (75 mL) cane sugar

½ teaspoon (2 mL) pure peppermint flavour

Coating

½ cup (125 mL) dairy-free dark chocolate chips

2 teaspoons (10 mL) pure mint flavouring

1. **Make the cookies:** Preheat the oven to 350°F (180°C). Line a baking sheet with parchment paper.

2. Melt the coconut oil and almond milk in a small saucepan over medium-low heat.

3. In a small bowl, stir together the almond flour, arrowroot powder, salt, and baking powder.

4. In a large bowl, mix together the cocoa powder, sugar, mint flavouring, and warmed coconut oil mixture until smooth. Then add the dry ingredients to the wet ingredients and mix until mostly combined. Switch to using your hands and form the mixture into a smooth dough.

5. Using a ½-ounce (14 g) cookie scoop or a 1-tablespoon (15 mL) measuring spoon, scoop the dough and shape and flatten it into 1 to 1½-inch (2.5 to 4 cm) rounds, ½ inch (1 cm) thick. Bake until the tops of the cookies are firm and dry to the touch, 9 to 10 minutes. (The cookies will firm up more as they cool.) Remove from the oven, then carefully lift the parchment paper with the cookies onto a rack and let cool completely.

recipe continues

6. **Make the coating and dip the cookies:** Line a baking sheet with parchment paper. When the cookies are cool, place the chocolate chips in a medium heatproof bowl set over a saucepan of simmering water (the bowl should not touch the water). Stir until the chocolate is melted and smooth. (Alternatively, in a small heat-resistant bowl, melt the chocolate in the microwave in 10-second intervals, stirring after each interval, 30 seconds total.) Stir in the peppermint flavour. Let cool for a few minutes so it thickens a bit.

7. Working one cookie at a time, dip the top of the cookie into the chocolate mint glaze to coat completely, letting excess chocolate drip back into the bowl. Place the cookie coated side up on the prepared baking sheet. Repeat with the remaining cookies. Transfer the baking sheet to the freezer and chill the cookies until the glaze is set, at least 15 minutes. Store the cookies in an airtight container in the fridge for up to 1 week or in the freezer for up to 1 month.

Tiramisu

Serves 8
Nut-Free
Vegan

Tiramisu is my all-time favourite dessert, which I discovered as a teenager roaming the streets of northern Italy. Deceptively simple, its layers of ladyfingers, soaked in espresso and stacked with mascarpone cream, is challenging to perfect, so it took me a long time to work up the nerve to create my own version. The result is an "I can't believe it's vegan" moment with layers of silken tofu cream, a nod to Japanese-Italian cuisine. Using good strong coffee is critical to the flavour of this dessert. If you don't have an espresso maker, try using double-strength coffee or good-quality instant espresso.

Mascarpone Cream

1 package (14 ounces/400 g) soft silken tofu, drained (about 2 cups)

1 cup (250 mL) 20 to 30% fat coconut cream

⅓ cup (75 mL) cane sugar

1 tablespoon (15 mL) pure vanilla extract

2 teaspoons (10 mL) freshly squeezed lemon juice

¼ teaspoon (1 mL) pure almond extract

¼ teaspoon (1 mL) salt

Sponge

1½ cups (375 mL) all-purpose flour

¾ teaspoon (3 mL) baking powder

¼ teaspoon (1 mL) baking soda

¼ teaspoon (1 mL) salt

¾ cup (175 mL) unsweetened oat milk

2 teaspoons (10 mL) pure vanilla extract

1 teaspoon (5 mL) apple cider vinegar

½ cup (125 mL) vegan stick butter (Earth Balance sticks are best for this recipe)

½ cup (125 mL) cane sugar

1. Preheat the oven to 350°F (180°C). Lightly grease a 9-inch (2.5 L) square cake pan. Line the pan with parchment paper with extra hanging over the sides.

2. **Make the mascarpone cream:** In a high-speed blender, combine the tofu, coconut cream, sugar, vanilla, lemon juice, almond extract, and salt. Blend on high speed until silky smooth, 1 minute. Pour into a small bowl, cover with plastic wrap, and chill in the fridge to thicken until ready to use.

3. **Meanwhile, prepare the sponge:** In a small bowl, stir together the flour, baking powder, baking soda, and salt.

4. In a glass measuring cup, stir together the oat milk, vanilla, and apple cider vinegar with a fork.

5. In a large bowl, cream together the butter and sugar using a handheld mixer. Pour in half of the oat milk mixture and mix well. Add a third of the flour mixture and the remaining oat milk mixture and beat well. Add the remaining flour mixture and gently fold in with a spatula until just combined. (The batter should look a bit thicker than a typical cake batter.)

recipe and ingredients continue

For assembly

¼ cup (60 mL) espresso or strongly brewed coffee

2 tablespoons (30 mL) coffee-flavoured liqueur, rum, or more espresso

Cocoa powder, for dusting

6. Scrape the batter into the prepared cake pan and smooth the top. Bake until lightly golden around the edges and a skewer inserted into the centre of the cake comes out clean, 21 to 24 minutes. Remove from the oven and let cool in the pan for 10 minutes, then carefully lift the cake onto a rack using the parchment paper over-hang and let cool completely.

7. **Assemble the tiramisu:** In a small bowl, stir together the espresso and liqueur.

8. Slice the cake into 12 ladyfingers (4 × 3 grid).

9. Remove the mascarpone cream from the fridge. Arrange 6 ladyfingers in the bottom of a 9 × 5-inch (2 L) loaf pan or a 2-quart (2 L) oval serving dish. Sprinkle half of the espresso mixture over the ladyfingers, then spread half of the mascarpone cream mixture evenly over top. Repeat the layers. Using a sifter, dust the top layer with the cocoa powder. Transfer to the fridge and chill until ready to serve. Store, covered, in the fridge for up to 4 days.

Mojito Granita

Serves 6

Gluten-Free

Low-FODMAP

Nut-Free

Vegan

3 cups (750 mL) water

½ cup (125 mL) cane sugar

Zest of 1 lime

½ cup (125 mL) freshly squeezed
lime juice (4 to 6 limes)

½ cup (125 mL) packed fresh
mint leaves

¼ cup (60 mL) rum (optional)

Granita is made from blended fruit and water, frozen and scraped with a fork to create mountains of delicate icy shavings. This granita is so fresh and juicy and flavourful, you might be surprised that something so good can be so easy to make. Inspired by the classic cocktail, the only effort required to make a granita is a little patience, but it's well worth it. This is a light and refreshing dessert for a hot day, and you'll want to make it again and again.

1. In a blender, combine the water, sugar, lime zest, lime juice, mint, and rum, if using. Blend for 20 to 30 seconds.

2. Pour the mixture into a 9-inch (2.5 L) square metal pan and transfer to the freezer to chill for 1 hour.

3. Remove the pan from the freezer and scrape a fork across the entire surface to break up the chunks of ice. Pop it back in the freezer and scrape every hour over a 4- to 6-hour period, until the entire mixture has been transformed into icy flakes similar to shaved ice. If not serving the same day, cover the pan and store in the freezer for up to 1 week.

Monster Cookies

Makes 20 cookies
Gluten-Free Option
Low-FODMAP Option
Vegan

Don't call these breakfast cookies—these cookies are sweeter and packed with straight up candy. My mother-in-law, Wendy, first introduced me to this treat, which has long been a holiday staple in our home. Minus the half-dozen eggs in her original recipe, this vegan version has a softer and even more decadent texture, but it means you have to handle the cookies carefully until they have fully cooled. Once you've tasted one, you'll realize what a difficult task waiting is, but it's well worth it!

½ cup (125 mL) warm water

¼ cup (60 mL) ground flaxseed

2 cups (500 mL) well-stirred natural peanut butter

⅔ cup (150 mL) pure maple syrup

1 teaspoon (5 mL) pure vanilla extract

2½ cups (625 mL) regular or gluten-free old-fashioned rolled oats

½ cup (125 mL) hemp hearts

2 teaspoons (10 mL) baking powder

½ teaspoon (2 mL) salt

⅓ cup (75 mL) dairy-free mini dark chocolate chips

⅓ cup (75 mL) vegan plain or peanut candy-coated chocolate candies (such as Unreal or No No's)

1. Preheat the oven to 350°F (180°C). Line a baking sheet with parchment paper.

2. In a large bowl, whisk together the water and flaxseed. Let sit for 5 minutes. Whisk in the peanut butter, maple syrup, and vanilla until smooth. Sprinkle in the rolled oats, hemp hearts, baking powder, and salt and mix thoroughly to combine. Fold in the chocolate chips and candies.

3. Using wet hands, scoop about ¼ cup (60 mL) of dough per cookie and roll and shape into firm discs, about 2½ inches (6 cm) in diameter and ¾ inch (2 cm) in height. Place the dough balls on the prepared baking sheet, evenly spaced, and bake until the tops are dry and golden, 13 to 16 minutes. (The cookies don't spread.) Remove from the oven, transfer the baking sheet to a rack, and let the cookies cool completely. If the cookies crack, you can gently press them together while they are still warm but otherwise don't touch them. They will not firm up until cool. Store, loosely covered, on the counter for up to 4 days or in an airtight container in the freezer for up to 1 month.

Swaps + Stuff

For a gluten-free version, use gluten-free rolled oats.

One cookie is a low-FODMAP serving.

Peach and Thyme Summer Crisp

Serves 6

Gluten-Free Option
Low-FODMAP Option
Nut-Free
Vegan

If forced to choose, I'll vote team crisp (or crumble!) over team pie any day. Crisps are so easy to make and don't mask the ripe, juicy fruit with excess pastry. Growing up, rhubarb crisp was a mainstay, so I thought it would be fun to create variations (see below) so you can whip up a nourishing dessert with seasonal fruit any time of year the craving strikes.

Fruit Mixture

2 pounds (900 g) ripe peaches (about 6 medium peaches), pitted and cut into ½-inch-thick (1 cm) slices

3 tablespoons (45 mL) cane sugar (see Note)

1 tablespoon (15 mL) arrowroot powder

1 tablespoon (15 mL) freshly squeezed lemon juice

2 teaspoons (10 mL) chopped fresh thyme leaves

Crisp Topping

¾ cup (175 mL) old-fashioned rolled oats

½ cup (125 mL) hemp hearts

⅓ cup (75 mL) spelt or gluten-free all-purpose flour

½ teaspoon (2 mL) baking powder

½ teaspoon (2 mL) cinnamon

¼ teaspoon (1 mL) salt

¼ cup (60 mL) extra-virgin olive, avocado, or melted coconut oil

¼ cup (60 mL) pure maple syrup

1 teaspoon (5 mL) pure vanilla extract

1. Preheat the oven to 350°F (180°C). Line a 9-inch (2.5 L) square baking dish with parchment paper or lightly grease a 9-inch (23 cm) cast-iron skillet.

2. **Prepare the fruit mixture:** In a medium bowl, combine the peaches, sugar, arrowroot, lemon juice, and thyme and toss the mixture with your hands to ensure that the fruit is evenly coated. Scrape the mixture into the prepared baking dish. Wipe the bowl.

3. **Prepare the crisp topping and bake:** In the same bowl, stir together the rolled oats, hemp hearts, spelt flour, baking powder, cinnamon, and salt. Add the olive oil, maple syrup, and vanilla and stir until well blended.

4. Spread the crisp topping evenly over the fruit. Bake until the topping is golden brown and the fruit mixture is bubbly and soft, 45 to 60 minutes. Remove from the oven and let cool for 10 minutes. Serve warm or at room temperature. Store leftovers, loosely covered, on the counter for up to 2 days or in the fridge for up to 4 days.

Seasonal Variations

Fall: Replace the peaches and thyme with 2 pounds (900 g) pears, cored and cut into ½-inch (1 cm) slices + 1 tablespoon (15 mL) grated peeled fresh ginger.

variations continue

Winter: Replace the peaches and thyme with 2 pounds (900 g) apples, cored and cut into ½-inch (1 cm) slices + 1 cup (250 mL) dried fruit, chopped + ¼ teaspoon (1 mL) ground cardamom + ¼ teaspoon (1 mL) ground cloves. (Use any dried fruit, such as figs, prunes, cranberries, or apricots. Soak in hot water for 10 minutes if not plump, drain, and gently squeeze out excess water before chopping.)

Spring: Replace the peaches with a combined total of 2 pounds (900 g) rhubarb, trimmed and cut into ½-inch (1 cm) slices + strawberries, hulled and halved or sliced. Increase the sugar to ⅓ cup (75 mL).

Note: Always taste your fruit before adding the sugar. If the fruit isn't at its sweetest, you might want to add an extra 1 tablespoon (15 mL) of sugar.

Swaps + Stuff

For gluten-free or low-FODMAP versions, use gluten-free rolled oats and flour (ensure no legume flours).

The rhubarb strawberry variation is low-FODMAP.

Feeling Good Is Your Birthright

Most of us are far too caught up in the doing/achieving part of life. I am very good at putting my head down and working my tail off and not even asking myself how I'm feeling.

If there is something that living through a global pandemic has taught me, it's that I want to have fun. I want to feel good. Life is too short not to make these things a priority. Here is a non-exhaustive list of things that make me feel really good:

- Feeling the sun on my skin
- Having just finished a run (note that I did not say the run itself)
- Cuddling with my kids
- Drinking lots of water
- Singing in the car
- Taking a hot Epsom salt bath after I tuck my kids into bed
- Eating something very delicious
- Having a good stretch
- Reading a good book
- Getting into a bed piled with blankets on a chilly night
- Letting loose a belly laugh
- Listening to music
- Hearing that my work helped someone feel better
- Experiencing that time when you're out with friends having a really good meal and, for a moment, you're so present and notice that everything—the music, the food, the conversation—is just perfect

I think one of the reasons why I love food so much is that it taught me, from a very early age, to welcome in pleasure for pleasure's sake. For a few moments, or longer if I'm lucky, I am out of my head and enjoying tastes and smells and textures just because I can. And this can happen multiple times per day. Sign me up! Because, as I said, I'm very good at just working so dang much. And things only got more intense after I had kids because suddenly I realized that my love for these tiny humans was so big that it could swallow me whole. I felt like I had to decide what I really wanted out of life and work very hard to achieve it, because I didn't want to wake up out of a haze twenty years later wondering what the heck had happened. But of course, that meant working even harder. Work is both my Achilles heel and my coping mechanism. And between entrepreneurship and parenting, it can be easy to forget that you're supposed to do things that make you feel good.

Now that I've remembered, I'm ready to make up for lost time. No matter what else is going on, food has always been one of the consistent sources of pleasure in my life. Like eating a whole bag of passionfruit on my hotel room floor in Sydney. Stealing bites of raw sweet bread dough from loaves rising under an old bedsheet on my avo's (grandmother's) kitchen table. Discovering alfajores in Buenos Aires and making it my mission to eat them daily. Cuddling under the covers with a bag of spicy dill potato chips on movie night. There is no world in which any of this isn't absolutely good for us. It's not an acceptable indulgence. It's part of creating a nourishing life.

It may seem a little obvious when you see it on paper, but perhaps you feel the same way about accepting pleasure in your life that I do. Maybe you've let it slip. Maybe you've deprioritized yourself. So maybe let's decide, right here and now, that together we'll choose pleasure. A slow morning with a cup of tea and a cozy blanket. The most delicious brownie—perhaps more than one. An afternoon spent in the sun with zero agenda and nothing to Instagram.

It's time to write your own list because you were designed to feel good. It is your birthright.

Carrot Cake with Cashew Frosting

Makes one 2-layer round cake

Gluten-Free

Vegan

Before there was tiramisu, carrot cake occupied the top spot in my dessert hall of fame. And of course, I have opinions about it. The cake should be moist, with a very tender crumb, and packed with carrots. I don't love nuts and raisins, but I can respect them, so you've got the option to add them here. And always cream cheese icing. Since the flavour of store-bought vegan cream cheese varies widely, I have created a cream cheese–inspired cashew frosting.

Cashew Frosting

1 cup (250 mL) cashews, soaked in boiling water for 30 minutes and drained

½ cup (125 mL) canned full-fat coconut milk

3 tablespoons (45 mL) pure maple syrup

2 tablespoons (30 mL) freshly squeezed lemon juice

2 tablespoons (30 mL) coconut oil

1 teaspoon (5 mL) pure vanilla extract

⅛ teaspoon (0.5 mL) salt

Carrot Cake

1½ cups (375 mL) almond flour

1½ cups (375 mL) gluten-free flour blend

2 teaspoons (10 mL) baking powder

2 teaspoons (10 mL) cinnamon

1 teaspoon (5 mL) baking soda

½ teaspoon (2 mL) salt

1. **Make the cashew frosting:** In a high-speed blender, combine the drained cashews, coconut milk, maple syrup, lemon juice, coconut oil, vanilla, and salt. Blend on low speed, then slowly increase to medium-high until smooth, 1 minute. Scrape the frosting into an airtight container and transfer to the fridge to firm up for at least 1 hour before using. The frosting can be stored in the fridge for up to 4 days.

2. **Meanwhile, make the carrot cake:** Preheat the oven to 350°F (180°C). Lightly grease two 8-inch (1.2 L) round cake pans with butter or coconut oil and line with rounds of parchment paper to fit the bottom of the pans for easier removal.

3. In a large bowl, stir together the almond flour, gluten-free flour blend, baking powder, cinnamon, baking soda, and salt.

recipe and ingredients continue

2 cups (500 mL) firmly packed grated carrots (about 2 large carrots)

1 cup (250 mL) unsweetened applesauce

½ cup (125 mL) extra-virgin olive or avocado oil

¾ cup (175 mL) cane sugar

½ cup (125 mL) unsweetened oat milk

¼ cup (60 mL) ground flaxseed

1 tablespoon (15 mL) apple cider vinegar

1 teaspoon (5 mL) pure vanilla extract

1 teaspoon (5 mL) grated peeled fresh ginger

½ cup (125 mL) raw pecans or walnuts, chopped (optional)

½ cup (125 mL) raisins (any type; optional)

4. In a medium bowl, mix together the carrots, applesauce, olive oil, sugar, oat milk, flaxseed, apple cider vinegar, vanilla, and ginger. Add the wet ingredients to the dry ingredients and stir to combine. Fold in the nuts and raisins, if using.

5. Scrape the batter into the prepared cake pans. Bake until the tops are firm and dry to the touch, the cakes are golden brown around the edges, and a skewer inserted into the centre of the cakes comes out clean, 33 to 37 minutes. Remove from the oven and let cool in the pans for 10 minutes, then carefully (the cakes will be soft) invert the cakes onto a rack and cool completely. Unfrosted cake layers can be stored, tightly wrapped, on the counter for up to 2 days.

6. **Assemble the cake:** Remove the cashew frosting from the fridge.

7. Place 1 cake layer top side up on a cake plate. Using an offset spatula, spread one third of the frosting over the cake layer to the edge.

8. Carefully set the second cake layer bottom side up on top of the frosted layer and spread one third of the frosting over it. Use the remaining frosting to frost the sides. Store the frosted cake, covered, in the fridge for up to 4 days. (Once the cake is iced, it must be kept refrigerated until ready to serve or the frosting will melt.)

Grilled Pineapple with Toasted Coconut

Serves 4

Gluten-Free

Low-FODMAP

Nut-Free

Vegan

¼ cup (60 mL) unsweetened shredded coconut

1 ripe pineapple

2 tablespoons (30 mL) avocado oil

2 tablespoons (30 mL) brown sugar

½ teaspoon (2 mL) cinnamon

Pinch of salt

Dairy-free vanilla or coconut-flavoured ice cream, for serving (optional)

I feel like such a dietitian when I say that fruit is the ultimate dessert, but I don't think we appreciate what a treat it can be in all its fragrant, sweet, and juicy decadence. This grilled pineapple leans on the simplest of preparation to coax out another dimension of flavour, which is helpful when you don't live in Hawaii where you can get these beauties just down the road. It's a delicious treat on its own but go ahead and add a scoop of dairy-free ice cream if you want something more.

1. Preheat a grill to medium-high heat (500°F/260°C). Line a baking sheet with parchment paper.

2. **Toast the coconut:** Heat a small dry skillet over medium-low heat. Toss in the coconut and toast, stirring constantly, until golden brown, 2 to 3 minutes. Remove from the heat and transfer the coconut to a small bowl.

3. **Prepare the pineapple:** Trim the ends of the pineapple and cut away the peel and core. Cut the pineapple in half lengthwise, then cut each half crosswise into ½-inch (1 cm) slices. Place the pineapple on the prepared baking sheet.

4. In a small bowl, stir together the avocado oil, brown sugar, cinnamon, and salt. Brush both side of the pineapple slices with the sugar mixture.

5. **Grill the pineapple:** Place the pineapple slices on the hot grill, close the lid, and grill until golden grill marks appear, 3 to 5 minutes per side.

6. Serve the grilled pineapple topped with toasted coconut and a small scoop of ice cream, if desired. Store leftovers, with the coconut, in an airtight container in the fridge for up to 3 days.

Swaps + Stuff

1 cup (250 mL) of pineapple is a low-FODMAP serving.

Rocky Road Blender Brownies

Makes 16 brownies

Gluten-Free

Vegan

½ cup (125 mL) vegan mini marshmallows, divided

1 cup (250 mL) quartered cooked red beets (about 2 medium beets)

½ cup (125 mL) pure maple syrup

½ cup (125 mL) unsweetened oat or soy milk

⅓ cup (75 mL) extra-virgin olive or avocado oil

1 teaspoon (5 mL) pure vanilla extract

1 teaspoon (5 mL) apple cider vinegar

2 cups (500 mL) almond flour

½ cup (125 mL) gluten-free old-fashioned rolled oats

⅔ cup (150 mL) cocoa powder

¼ cup (60 mL) ground flaxseed

2 teaspoons (10 mL) baking powder

½ teaspoon (2 mL) salt

½ teaspoon (2 mL) cinnamon

⅓ cup (75 mL) chopped raw walnuts or walnut pieces

½ cup (125 mL) dairy-free mini dark chocolate chips, reserving 1 tablespoon (15 mL) for topping

I am the first to say that not everything you eat must be "healthy" for you to be healthy. Sometimes (plenty of times) I just want a dang potato chip. But I also really enjoy creating yummy treats that help you eat more plants, because when they taste this good, why not? No one will believe that these plush and fudgy brownies are made from beets and almonds. They are that good. If you've never cooked with vegan marshmallows before, note that they don't hold their shape the way regular marshmallows do but are every bit as tasty.

1. Preheat the oven to 350°F (180°C). Lightly grease a 9-inch (2.5 L) square baking pan. Line the pan with parchment paper with extra hanging over the sides.

2. Cut ¼ cup (60 mL) of the marshmallows in half and set aside.

3. In a high-speed blender, combine the beets, maple syrup, oat milk, olive oil, vanilla, and apple cider vinegar and blend on medium speed for 30 seconds until smooth. Add the almond flour, rolled oats, cocoa powder, flaxseed, baking powder, salt, and cinnamon. Blend on medium speed for 30 seconds, then increase the speed to medium-high and blend until smooth with no lumps, about another 30 seconds. Stir in the walnuts, the remaining ¼ cup (60 mL) whole marshmallows, and the chocolate chips.

4. Scrape the batter into the prepared baking pan and smooth the top. Scatter the halved marshmallows and the reserved 1 tablespoon (15 mL) chocolate chips evenly over the batter. Bake until the top is dry to the touch and the sides are starting to crack a bit, 42 to 48 minutes. Remove from the oven and let cool in the pan for 10 minutes, then carefully lift the brownies onto a rack using the parchment paper overhang and let cool completely. Store the brownies, loosely covered, on the counter for up to 4 days or tightly wrapped in the freezer for up to 1 month.

Cardamom Tahini Cookies with Apricots and Pistachios

If you like halva, the sesame-based sweet, you'll love these tahini cookies, studded with tender dried apricots and crunchy pistachios. This simple cookie punches way above its weight with a nutty, complex flavour laced with fragrant cardamom and clove. Bonus: they're so quick to make you could go from craving to snacking in 30 minutes flat.

Makes 2 dozen cookies

Nut-Free Option

Vegan

1 cup (250 mL) well-stirred tahini

⅓ cup (75 mL) pure maple syrup

3 tablespoons (45 mL) cane sugar

2 teaspoons (10 mL) pure vanilla extract

1 cup (250 mL) whole-grain spelt or whole wheat flour

½ teaspoon (2 mL) baking powder

½ teaspoon (2 mL) ground cardamom

½ teaspoon (2 mL) salt

⅛ teaspoon (0.5 mL) ground cloves

½ cup (125 mL) dried apricots, diced

⅓ cup (75 mL) pistachios, finely chopped, divided

1. Preheat the oven to 350°F (180°C). Line a baking sheet with parchment paper.

2. In a medium bowl, whisk together the tahini, maple syrup, sugar, and vanilla. Sprinkle in the spelt flour, baking powder, cardamom, salt, and cloves. Stir to combine until a soft dough forms and no dry patches remain. Fold in the apricots and half of the pistachios.

3. Place the remaining pistachios in a small bowl.

4. Scoop a rounded tablespoon (15 mL) of dough per cookie into a ball, and gently press the top of the ball into the bowl of pistachios. Place the cookies nut side up on the prepared baking sheet, evenly spaced. Bake until set and dry to the touch, 14 to 15 minutes.

5. Remove from the oven and let cool on the baking sheet for 10 minutes, then transfer the cookies to a rack and let cool completely. Store in an airtight container on the counter for up to 5 days or in the freezer for up to 1 month.

Swaps + Stuff

For a nut-free version, swap the pistachios for chopped raw pumpkin seeds or sesame seeds.

Mini Cashew Cheesecakes

Makes 12 mini cheesecakes

Gluten-Free

Vegan

I make cashew cheesecakes so often they're practically a food group in my house! It's the kind of plant-based treat that perfectly highlights the magic of using whole foods to create something totally new. For this variation, I've swirled the cashew cream with a Miso Caramel Sauce (page 298) for a salted caramel vibe, but if you're looking for something a bit extra, go ahead and top them with a bit of flaky sea salt before freezing.

Crust

¾ cup (175 mL) hemp seeds

½ cup (125 mL) pitted Medjool dates

¼ cup (60 mL) unsweetened shredded coconut

1 teaspoon (5 mL) freshly grated lemon zest

1 teaspoon (5 mL) freshly squeezed lemon juice

½ teaspoon (2 mL) cinnamon

⅛ teaspoon (0.5 mL) salt

Filling

1½ cups (375 mL) raw cashews, soaked in hot water for at least 30 minutes, rinsed and drained

¾ cup (175 mL) coconut milk

¾ cup (175 mL) Miso Caramel Sauce (page 298), divided

3 tablespoons (45 mL) freshly squeezed lemon juice (about 1½ lemons)

1 tablespoon (15 mL) pure maple syrup

1 teaspoon (5 mL) pure vanilla extract

¼ teaspoon (1 mL) salt

1. Line a 12-cup muffin tin with paper liners.

2. **Prepare the crust:** In a food processor, combine the hemp seeds, dates, coconut, lemon zest, lemon juice, cinnamon, and salt. Pulse until the dates are finely chopped and the mixture is well combined. The mixture should stick together when pressed between 2 fingers.

3. Scoop a scant tablespoon (about 15 mL) of crust mixture into each muffin cup. Use the bottom of a ¼ cup (60 mL) measuring cup or your fingers to gently press the mixture into an even layer in the bottom of each muffin cup.

4. **Make the filling:** In a high-speed blender, combine the drained cashews, coconut milk, ½ cup (125 mL) of the miso caramel sauce, lemon juice, maple syrup, vanilla, and salt. Blend on high speed until silky smooth, 1 to 2 minutes.

5. **Fill and freeze the cheesecakes:** Pour equal portions of the filling into the muffin cups. Using a spoon, swirl 1 teaspoon (5 mL) of the remaining miso caramel sauce on top of each cheesecake. Cover the pan loosely with foil and freeze until set, at least 6 hours. Once frozen, the cheesecakes can be stored in an airtight container in the freezer for up to 1 week.

6. Remove the cheesecakes from the freezer and let sit for 5 minutes before serving.

10 Everyday Tonics + Potions

Salted Grapefruit Juice with Jalapeño

Makes about 2 cups (500 mL) juice

Gluten-Free

Nut-Free

Vegan

4 medium pink grapefruits

¼ teaspoon (1 mL) flaky sea salt

1 jalapeño pepper, thinly sliced

Ice cubes

Grapefruit juice, but fancy! I've made a concerted effort to drink fewer alcoholic beverages over the last few years, so I am constantly on a quest to find zero-proof options that still feel special. Freshly squeezed grapefruit juice, spiked with jalapeño and salt and served over ice, feels like a real cocktail, minus the hangover.

Before adding the jalapeño pepper, taste a tiny piece. Is it spicy or mild? Then you can decide how much jalapeño you want to use in your juice.

1. **Juice the grapefruits:** You can juice the grapefruits by hand or use a high-speed blender.

   If juicing by hand, pour the grapefruit juice into a 2-cup (500 mL) mason jar and stir in the flaky sea salt.

   If using a high-speed blender, cut away the peel and pith from the grapefruits. Toss the grapefruit into the blender and blend on high speed into a juice, about 30 seconds. Add the flaky sea salt and blend for a few more seconds. You can strain the juice if you like or skip (more fibre!).

2. **Assemble the drink:** Place 2 to 3 slices of jalapeño in a glass and muddle with a spoon. Add 2 or 3 ice cubes. Pour ½ cup (125 mL) of the salted grapefruit juice over the ice and stir. If not serving the juice right away, pour it into a 2-cup (500 mL) mason jar, toss in a few slices of jalapeño, screw on the lid, and store in the fridge. Note that the longer the juice sits, the more heat from the jalapeños will infuse the juice, so feel free to store the juice without the sliced jalapeño for up to 2 days. The juice will naturally separate; just shake before serving.

   Note: The grapefruit juice is super refreshing over ice, mixed fifty-fifty with sparkling water, or yes, as a base for cocktails with gin or mezcal.

Dandelion Vinegar

Makes about 1 cup (250 mL)

Gluten-Free

Nut-Free

Vegan

1 cup (250 mL) lightly packed dandelion blossoms

1 cup (250 mL) raw apple cider vinegar

Many of the plants we dismiss as weeds are in fact herbs that we'd be wise to consume, including the persistent and resilient dandelions that return to our lawns year after year. Their nutrient-dense leaves can be turned into pesto or sautéed like spinach, and the blossoms can be used to infuse a bit of sunshine into vinegar to enrich salad dressings and sauces. Always ensure that the area you are collecting from is free of lawn chemicals and not used by your furry friends as a litter box!

1. Rinse the dandelion blossoms well in a sieve. Gently pat dry with a clean kitchen towel. Place the blossoms in a clean 2-cup (500 mL) mason jar and pour the apple cider vinegar over top.

2. Place the jar in a cool, dark place and let sit for 1 week until the blossoms look wilted and discoloured and the vinegar darkens in colour. Taste; if you want it stronger, you can infuse for another week.

3. Strain the vinegar through a fine-mesh sieve into a small bowl and then return to the mason jar. Tightly screw on the lid and store in the fridge for up to 1 month. Sediment is normal; give it a gentle swirl before using.

Golden Berry Elixir

Makes about 2 cups (500 mL)

Gluten-Free

Nut-Free

Vegan

½ cup (125 mL) unsweetened dried golden berries

1 cup (250 mL) boiling water

1 cup (250 mL) freshly squeezed orange juice

1 (1-inch/2.5 cm) piece fresh ginger, peeled and grated

Ice cubes, for serving

Whether they are fresh or dried, I love golden berries. These tart little orbs that hail from the Andes mountains of South America are packed with energizing iron, and this elixir is sweet-tart and delightfully complex. Delicious served over ice, it feels like a treat for both body and soul.

1. Place the golden berries in a small heatproof bowl. Pour the boiling water over the golden berries and let soak for 1 hour. (Dried golden berries are very tough and need thorough hydration to blend well.)

2. Pour the golden berries and their soaking liquid into a high-speed blender. Add the orange juice and ginger. Blend on high speed until the juice is smooth with no chunks remaining, 1 minute. You can strain the juice through a fine-mesh sieve into a mason jar if you prefer a lighter texture, but I like it unstrained.

3. Serve over ice cubes. Store in a sealed mason jar in the fridge for up to 4 days. The elixir will separate, which is normal. Shake vigorously before using.

Hibiscus Lemonade

Makes 8 cups (2 L)

Gluten-Free

Nut-Free

Vegan

½ cup (125 mL) dried loose
    hibiscus flowers

¼ to ⅓ cup (60 to 75 mL) cane
    sugar, to taste

Pinch of salt

2 cups (500 mL) boiling water

1 cup (250 mL) freshly squeezed
    lemon juice (3 to 4 juicy
    lemons)

5 cups (1.25 L) cold water (or
    3 cups/750 mL water, plus
    2 heaping cups/500 mL ice
    cubes)

Sweet, tart hibiscus flowers are the perfect addition to lemonade, which for me, should be only lightly sweetened. If you usually find lemonade too sweet, you'll love this. I've included a few variations, in case you like your lemonade sparkling instead of still or have some Hibiscus Rose Syrup (page 287) on hand.

1. Place the hibiscus flowers, sugar, and salt in a 2-cup (500 mL) mason jar and stir. Pour the boiling water over the hibiscus mixture. Stir to dissolve the sugar and allow to steep for 15 minutes.

2. Strain the syrup through a fine-mesh sieve into a pitcher. Pour in the lemon juice and water (or water and ice combination to chill faster) and transfer to the fridge to chill before serving.

Variations

1. Combine the strained hibiscus syrup and lemon juice in the pitcher and chill for 1 hour. Add 5 cups (1.25 L) chilled sparkling water instead of the still water.

2. Another option is to add the lemon juice to 7 cups of water, use Hibiscus Rose Syrup (page 287), and sweeten to taste.

Spiced Chocolate Hemp Milk

Serves 4

Gluten-Free

Low-FODMAP Option

Nut-Free Option

Vegan

4 cups (1 L) water

½ cup (125 mL) hemp hearts

½ cup (125 mL) raw cacao or cocoa powder

¼ cup (60 mL) cashew, almond, or sunflower seed butter

1 teaspoon (5 mL) cinnamon

1 teaspoon (5 mL) pure vanilla extract

½ teaspoon (2 mL) ground cardamom

¼ teaspoon (1 mL) fennel seeds

¼ teaspoon (1 mL) cayenne pepper or red chili flakes

Pinch of salt

2 to 4 tablespoons (30 to 60 mL) pure maple syrup

Ice cubes, for serving

Love the idea of hemp hearts, but don't know what to do with them? Make this grown-up chocolate milk, which might just be the most delicious way to get your omega-3s in. It's at least a tie with my Brownie Batter Breakfast Toast (page 31). Flecked with cinnamon, cardamom, and fennel, it tastes similar to the chocolate milk you grew up with, but spicier. Ditch the cayenne and it is family friendly, if you're feeling generous enough to share.

1. In a high-speed blender, combine the water, hemp hearts, cacao powder, cashew butter, cinnamon, vanilla, cardamom, fennel seeds, cayenne pepper, salt, and the desired amount of maple syrup to a high-speed blender. (I recommend 2 tablespoons/30 mL maple syrup for a more unsweetened milk, or ¼ cup/60 mL for a lightly sweetened milk.) Blend on high speed until smooth, about 1 minute.

2. Immediately pour into glasses over ice cubes or add to warm drinks. Store in a tightly sealed bottle or mason jar in the fridge for up to 3 days. Natural plant milks will separate as they sit, which is normal and not an indication of spoilage. Shake vigorously before using.

Swaps + Stuff

For a nut-free version, use sunflower seed butter.

For a low-FODMAP version, use almond butter.

You Are Nature

Plants are magic. The more I work with them, the more I learn about them, the more I welcome them into my life, the more I feel it.

Even though I had been vegetarian for a while, it wasn't until I got serious about eating more actual plants that I started to feel a shift inside my body. It was as if a source of energy that I hadn't previously been able to access had been tapped. It felt joyful. It felt like the beginning of something, and I guess it was, given where I am today. It is not an overstatement to say that plants changed my health and my life for the better, so I will take any opportunity I can to spend more time with them, whether that's eating, learning, cooking, or growing all of the things.

Despite my clear fanaticism for plants, and growing up around a garden as a child, gardening does not come naturally to me. I'm not one of those people with "skills." Sure, I can cook, but I'm talking about those folks who somehow know how to change a tire, fluently speak another language, build a canoe, or whatever. I am very much not that person! So when I found myself with a little bit of space to plant some veg, I had a lot to learn and I did so, most often, with a gardening glove on one hand and my phone in the other. Early attempts at starting seeds indoors failed miserably, so I either buy a start or direct sow my seeds when the weather is right. I learned to get over my distaste for creepy-crawly things fast because, holy heck, I cannot believe the epic insect menagerie that is our yard.

Properly maintaining a sizeable garden is the world's most time-consuming hobby; I had thought it was knitting, which I had abandoned long ago for that same reason, but it's actually gardening. Which means that some years—like, say, when I'm writing a book—my garden looks a wee bit neglected. And yet, because nature is so damn magical, it still yields enough of a harvest that I can wholeheartedly recommend you give it a try: 10/10, like and subscribe.

If the idea of gardening seems intimidating, or space isn't on your side, all you really need to get started is a sunny window and a couple of small pots. At the risk of sounding like a dietitian cliché, just growing some basil or mint will help you form a deeper connection to the plant world. It will also help you avoid buying those tiny clamshells of herbs that are always more than you need for one recipe so they languish in the back of your fridge, growing mould.

Herbs are also a beautiful entry into the world of plant medicines, which have been sustaining humans since our arrival on this planet. I have been interested in herbalism for as long as I have nutrition. Herbs hold a ton of bioactive compounds that support human health—and also a connection to our cultural lineages around interacting with the natural world. Ask your grandmother about that concoction she used to make you when you were sick, or tap your uncle for his fermentation secrets. And if you're looking to dive deeper, books like *Braiding Sweetgrass* by Robin Wall Kimmerer, *Held by the Land* by Leigh Joseph, and *Plants for the People* by Erin Lovell Verinder are excellent entries into the world of plant medicines.

We humans like to think we're top of the heap and praise ourselves in our ability to bend our environment to our wills. I'm not sure that's working out so well for us, given our current climate crisis. Perhaps it's time to embrace the fact that we are not just a part of nature, but nature itself. Every cell of your body has its origins in nature, and the food we choose to eat is the most direct connection between us and the rest of this glorious ecosystem. Plants create energy from sunlight and draw nutrients up through the soil—soil that is a living, breathing organism teeming with microbes. Your body disassembles those nutrients and uses them to build each and every one of the enzymes, muscle fibres, and bones you call home. The oxygen you breathe is carried throughout your body and delivered to your cells to help you create energy. And the carbon dioxide you breathe out is received by plants.

This isn't just romantic hyperbole. You are literally made of nature, and food powers your life force. So many try to use our food choices as a way of delineating and dividing us—you're paleo, I'm vegan—but in fact, food brings us closer together than we realize. Think of the dinner you'll make tonight: it was grown in soil composed of organisms long since passed and tended by the hands of someone you may never meet, but in eating that bunch of kale, or those almonds, you have a direct line of connection to that place and that person. Many people, in fact. Don't forget to wash that dang produce.

I truly believe that the future is plants. Everyone—from my mom to my previously carnivorous best friend to Michelin-star chefs—is getting into plant-based eating, even if they're not actually going vegan. In fact, it's thought that less than 1 percent of the world population is fully vegan. I'm all for this plant curiosity because we'll do far more for our collective personal health, animal agriculture, and sustainability if we all shift our diets in the direction of plants as opposed to just a few of us going fully vegan. You don't have to put a label on it, just eat more plants.

Our food choices have an impact, on people, on animals, and on the planet. According to a paper published in 2019 in the journal *Sustainability*, 44 percent of global methane production is attributable to livestock. Meat and cheese production may comprise 40 percent of daily greenhouse gas emissions. We have the power to make choices that protect our environment and therefore safeguard our own future here on this planet. And plants can help us do just that. I simply want to create food for anyone who wants to eat plants, whenever they want to eat them. Wherever you're at, it's all good, whether you eat nothing but plants or are simply trying to eat more of them.

Fermented Blueberry Chamomile Shrub

Makes 2 cups (500 mL) syrup

Gluten-Free

Nut-Free

Vegan

1 cup (250 mL) raw apple cider vinegar

½ cup (125 mL) cane sugar

2 cups (500 mL) fresh or frozen blueberries (if using fresh berries, cut in half)

¼ cup (60 mL) dried whole chamomile flowers (or 2 tablespoons/30 mL chamomile loose tea leaves)

Soda water, for serving

In case you think I'm talking greenery, a shrub is actually a sweetened drinking vinegar made from fruit. Using raw apple cider vinegar as your base allows you to create a ferment with endless variations. I love the combination of antioxidant-rich blueberries and chamomile, a nervine herb used for generations whenever you need a sense of calm.

1. Wash a 4-cup (1 L) mason jar well with hot, soapy water and dry with a clean kitchen towel.

2. Pour the apple cider vinegar and sugar into the mason jar and stir. (It is okay if the sugar doesn't fully dissolve; it will dissolve as the shrub ferments.) Add the blueberries and chamomile to the jar. Tightly screw on the lid and gently shake to coat the berries in the mixture. Let sit in a warm place in your kitchen, away from direct sunlight, for 1 to 2 weeks until the sugar is completely dissolved and the shrub tastes sweet and a bit tart to your liking. Give it a stir daily with a wooden spoon.

3. Strain the shrub through a fine-mesh strainer into a clean 2-cup (500 mL) mason jar. Tightly screw on the lid and store in the fridge for up to 1 month. (You can rinse the chamomile off the fermented berries, then store the berries in an airtight container in the fridge for up to 3 days. Use in salads or grain bowls.)

4. To serve, pour 2 tablespoons (30 mL) of the shrub into a tall glass. Top with soda water.

Pomegranate Ginger Syrup

**Makes about 1 cup
(250 mL)**

Gluten-Free

Nut-Free

Vegan

2 cups (500 mL) fresh 100%
pomegranate juice (such as
POM Wonderful; see Note)

⅓ cup (75 mL) peeled and
chopped fresh ginger

2 tablespoons (30 mL) pure
maple syrup

I'm really embracing syrups as I venture into the world of non-alcoholic drinks. I'm not big on sweet drinks, so my mission is to create syrups that have lots of flavour so that a little syrup is all you need. This one fits the bill quite nicely. Pomegranate juice is an antioxidant powerhouse, and its bold flavour pairs beautifully with spicy ginger in this syrup. I like to keep this on hand to flavour sparkling water when I need something that feels a little special.

1. In a small saucepan, combine the pomegranate juice, ginger, and maple syrup. Bring to a boil over high heat, then reduce the heat to medium and simmer, uncovered, until the liquid is reduced by half, 30 to 35 minutes. Remove from the heat and let the syrup cool completely in the pot. Strain the syrup through a fine-mesh sieve into a 2-cup (500 mL) mason jar. Discard the ginger. Tightly screw on the lid and store in the fridge for up to 2 weeks.

2. To use, add 1 to 2 tablespoons (15 to 30 mL) of the syrup to a tall glass of soda water or use to sweeten brewed or iced teas.

   Note: If you don't have access to fresh pomegranate juice, you can also use shelf-stable 100% pomegranate juice but it will not be as flavourful.

Hibiscus Rose Syrup

Makes about ½ cup (125 mL)

Gluten-Free

Nut-Free

Vegan

⅔ cup (150 mL) cane sugar

½ cup (125 mL) water

¼ cup (60 mL) dried loose hibiscus flowers (or 2 tablespoons/30 mL pure hibiscus tea leaves)

2 tablespoons (30 mL) rose water

Hibiscus flowers, also known as Jamaica flowers, are common in tropical and subtropical climates the world over and make a beautiful nutrient-dense tea rich in vitamin C. Paired with calming rose, this syrup is lovely as a sparkling cocktail or to sweeten desserts. I like to add a splash to sparkling water on a warm evening to help me wind down.

1. In a small saucepan, combine the sugar, water, and hibiscus flowers. Bring to a boil over medium heat, and stir until the sugar is dissolved. Remove from the heat and allow the tea to steep for 1 hour.

2. Strain the tea through a fine-mesh sieve into a 1-cup (250 mL) mason jar (see Note). Add the rose water, screw the lid on tightly, and store in the fridge for up to 1 week.

3. To use, stir 1 to 2 tablespoons (15 to 30 mL) of the syrup into a tall glass of soda water or use to sweeten brewed or iced teas.

Note: Don't throw away your steeped hibiscus! Instead, use this tip I learned from my friend Gabriel: freeze the dried flowers on a sheet of parchment paper, then transfer them to a freezer bag. Use in smoothies, energy balls, or enchiladas.

Sniffle Soother

**Makes ten ¼-cup (60 mL)
shots**
Gluten-Free
Low-FODMAP Option
Nut-Free
Vegan

When you're sick, anything that makes you feel better is welcome . . . especially when you don't have much of an appetite. This wellness shot is packed with fiery ginger, which helps alleviate nausea due to its prokinetic actions as well as being a known anti-inflammatory. Garlic is anti-microbial, and the heat of this wellness shot will definitely get the nose running, to help you beat that annoying stuffi-ness of cold season. If the garlic freaks you out, there is still lots of goodness to be had, so make a garlic-free batch and freeze it for the next time sniffles get you down—it makes a nice base for a warm tonic (see Note).

1½ cups (375 mL) water

1 unpeeled orange, ends
    trimmed and quartered

½ heaping cup (125 mL) peeled
    and chopped fresh ginger

1 (2-inch/5 cm) piece fresh
    turmeric, peeled

1 clove garlic

Freshly cracked black pepper

Pinch of cayenne pepper

Pinch of salt

1. In a high-speed blender, combine the water, orange, ginger, turmeric, garlic, black pepper, cayenne pepper, and salt. Blend on high speed until smooth and frothy, 1 minute. (You can strain the mixture through a fine-mesh sieve into a small bowl for a smoother texture, but I don't.)

2. Pour the mixture into a 2-cup (500 mL) mason jar and tightly screw on the lid. Store in the fridge for up to 3 days. (Alternatively, pour into ice cube compartments and freeze the tray for up to 1 month.)

3. Drink the sniffle soother as a ¼-cup (60 mL) shot.

   Note: For a warm tonic, make a garlic-free sniffle soother. Add ¼ cup (60 mL) or 3 frozen cubes of the garlic-free soother to a mug and cover with hot water.

   Swaps + Stuff
   For a low-FODMAP version, omit the garlic.

Cardamom Dandy Coffee

Serves 1

Gluten-Free

Nut-Free

Vegan

1 cup (250 mL) of your favourite unsweetened non-dairy nut-free milk (I like oat milk)

¼ teaspoon (1 mL) ground cardamom

1 teaspoon (5 mL) cocoa or raw cacao powder

1 pitted Medjool date or pure maple syrup, to taste

1½ teaspoons (7 mL) Dandy Blend powder (see Note)

I love coffee, but my nervous system, not so much. Luckily, there are a lot of coffee alternatives out there, and my favourite is probably Dandy Blend instant herbal beverage, a very old-school hippie concoction made from—you guessed it—dandelion root. Paired with cardamom, this caffeine-free mocha-ish concoction is deeply satisfying, and since it has no caffeine, you can enjoy it all day long.

1. In a small saucepan, combine the milk, cardamom, cocoa powder, and date over medium-low heat. Once steaming, remove from the heat.

2. Add the Dandy Blend powder, then using an immersion blender, blend until smooth. Pour into a mug and serve. (Alternatively, you can combine all the ingredients in a high-speed blender and blend on the soup setting to blend and heat at the same time.)

Note: I like Dandy Blend best here for flavour, but you could also make this drink with instant espresso or dandelion root granules.

11

Staples That Make Anything Better

Simple Za'atar

Makes ⅓ cup (75 mL)
Gluten-Free
Low-FODMAP
Nut-Free
Vegan

Za'atar is a spice blend native to the Eastern Mediterranean, where a variety of wild oregano, called za'atar or hyssop, thrives in the arid landscape. This is a simplified version, with just five ingredients to help you recreate this incredible spice blend at home. Keep on hand at all times; it will make almost anything you eat taste better.

4 teaspoons (20 mL) ground sumac

4 teaspoons (20 mL) dried oregano

4 teaspoons (20 mL) sesame seeds

2 teaspoons (10 mL) dried thyme

1 teaspoon (5 mL) salt

1. In a small jar with a lid, combine the sumac, oregano, sesame seeds, thyme, and salt. Screw on the lid and gently shake to combine. Store at room temperature for up to 6 months.

Quick Pickled Red Onions

Makes about 1½ cups (375 mL)
Gluten-Free
Nut-Free
Vegan

I've never met a pickle I didn't like, and pickled onions are no exception. Onions are deeply nutrient-dense vegetables, packed with fermentable carbohydrates that boost gut health and a host of phytochemicals such as quercetin. Pickling allows onions' complex flavour to shine so they can claim a bit of the vegetable spotlight. A bit salty, a bit tangy, and completely delicious on everything from sandwiches to grain bowls to tacos.

½ cup (125 mL) apple cider vinegar or white wine vinegar

½ cup (125 mL) water

1 tablespoon (15 mL) cane sugar

1 teaspoon (5 mL) salt

1 medium red onion, peeled and thinly sliced

1. In a small saucepan, combine the apple cider vinegar, water, sugar, and salt over medium heat, stirring until the sugar is completely dissolved. Let cool for 5 minutes.

2. Place the sliced red onions in a 2-cup (500 mL) mason jar. Carefully pour the vinegar mixture over the onions. Loosely cover and let cool to room temperature on the counter. The pickled onions are ready to eat after 1 hour. Screw on the lid tightly and store in the fridge for up to 1 week.

Spicy Cilantro Garlic Sauce

Makes about 1 cup (250 mL)

Gluten-Free

Nut-Free

Vegan

I love a green sauce, whether it's zhug, chermoula, or chimichurri, which this recipe replicates most closely. What do they all have in common? Plenty of fresh green herbs, often cilantro, which is highly underrated in terms of its nutritional value. Fresh herbs are packed with volatile oils and antioxidant phytochemicals, plus they are an inexpensive way to get more greens into your life.

2 cups (500 mL) firmly packed fresh cilantro leaves and tender stems

2 cloves garlic

½ to 1 jalapeño pepper, depending on desired heat, roughly chopped

Juice of 1 lime

2 tablespoons (30 mL) extra-virgin olive or avocado oil

1 tablespoon (15 mL) apple cider vinegar

½ teaspoon (2 mL) salt

1. In a food processor, combine the cilantro, garlic, jalapeño, lime juice, olive oil, apple cider vinegar, and salt. Pulse until the mixture looks like a loose pesto. Taste and adjust the salt if needed. (I usually add another pinch or so.) Store in an airtight container in the fridge for up to 5 days.

Roasted Red Pepper Relish

Makes about 1¼ cups (300 mL)

Gluten-Free

Nut-Free

Vegan

There is always a jar of roasted red peppers in my fridge. I will layer them on sandwiches, wraps, and roasted veggies; pile them on a grain or hummus bowl like my Coriander Chili Hummus Bowl (page 223); or blend them into dips. They've got so much flavour and are an easy way to add more plants to your plate.

1½ cups (375 mL) jarred roasted red peppers

¼ large red onion, roughly chopped

1 clove garlic

1 tablespoon (15 mL) red wine vinegar

1 tablespoon (15 mL) pure maple syrup

1 teaspoon hot sauce, plus more to taste (I use Valentina extra hot)

½ teaspoon (2 mL) salt, plus more for seasoning

Freshly cracked black pepper

Squeeze of lime juice

1. Drain the roasted red peppers. Place between a few layers of paper towel and gently press down to remove excess liquid to avoid making the relish too watery.

2. In a small food processor, combine the red peppers, red onions, garlic, red wine vinegar, maple syrup, hot sauce, salt, and black pepper to taste. Pulse until a loose relish forms. Taste, add a squeeze of lime juice, and adjust the salt (this can help minimize any bitterness from the red peppers) and hot sauce as needed. Store in an airtight container in the fridge for up to 5 days.

Cashew Tzatziki

**Makes about 2 cups
(500 mL)**

Gluten-Free

Vegan

1¼ cups (300 mL) raw cashews, soaked in boiling water for 30 minutes, drained

½ cup (125 mL) water

¼ cup (60 mL) freshly squeezed lemon juice

2 cloves garlic, grated on a microplane

¾ teaspoon (3 mL) salt, plus more for seasoning

½ teaspoon (2 mL) garlic powder

2 cups (500 mL) packed grated English cucumber, squeezed (1 medium cucumber)

¼ cup (60 mL) lightly packed fresh dill, finely chopped

Freshly cracked black pepper, to taste

Tzatziki is a classic Greek dip made from yogurt, but I find that cashews do quite nicely as a vegan alternative. You could use this as a dip for the Spicy Tofu Nuggets (page 240) or even the Black Olive and Za'atar Focaccia (page 224), but I also love it straight up with some pita and veggies as a light snack-style lunch.

1. In a high-speed blender, combine the drained cashews, water, lemon juice, garlic, salt, and garlic powder. Starting on medium speed and slowly increasing to high-speed for 1 full minute, blend until smooth. Stop occasionally to scrape down the sides of the bowl.

2. Scrape the tzatziki into a small bowl. Stir in the cucumber and dill. Cover with plastic wrap and transfer to the fridge to chill for 1 hour so the flavours have time to meld. Taste and adjust the salt, pepper, or lemon juice as needed. Store in an airtight container in the fridge for up to 4 days. Give it a stir before using.

Simple Preserved Lemons

Makes about 2 cups (500 mL)

Gluten-Free

Low-FODMAP

Nut-Free

Vegan

Preserved lemons are so simple to make and add such an alluring flavour to soups and stews like my Lemony Chickpea and Potato Stew (page 214), dips like my Coriander Chili Hummus Bowl (page 223), or rice dishes. The secret? A little goes a long way, so ensure that when you use them, you scrape away all the soft flesh (it's too salty!) and give it a quick rinse in water. I promise, there will still be plenty of flavour left.

4 lemons

3 tablespoons (45 mL) coarse salt, divided

Optional Add-Ins (choose 2 or 3)

1 star anise

½ cinnamon stick

1 bay leaf

½ teaspoon (2 mL) black peppercorns

½ teaspoon (2 mL) coriander seeds

1. Have ready a very clean 2-cup (500 mL) mason jar.

2. Juice 2 of the lemons.

3. Wash and dry the remaining 2 lemons. Slice a bit from the ends to flatten. Using a sharp knife, quarter the lemons lengthwise, leaving the bottom ½ inch (1 cm) intact. Using a spoon, place 1 tablespoon (15 mL) of the salt into each lemon. Pack the lemons into the mason jar with a pestle or clean hands to help release the juice. Add desired spice add-ins. Top with the remaining 1 tablespoon (15 mL) salt and press down again. Let the jar sit on the counter for 1 hour, then press down on the lemons again. Add enough of the lemon juice to ensure that the lemons are completely submerged. Loosely screw on the lid and leave on the counter for 30 days to cure. You can cure the lemons for much longer if you wish, up to 3 months. Check the lemons daily, ensuring that they stay submerged in liquid by pressing down on them with a clean spoon as needed.

4. When the skins are translucent, the lemons are ready to use. Transfer to the fridge for up to 6 months. To use, scrape away the flesh and pith, leaving the skin intact. Rinse off extra salt with water. Dice peels to add to recipes.

Herbed Cashew Cheese

Makes about 1½ cups (375 mL)

Gluten-Free

Vegan

This thick and spreadable cashew cheese is packed with fragrant herbs and delicious on everything from crackers to sandwiches to pizza! Because this recipe makes a big batch, I've given you lots of ways to use it up, including the West Coast Hippie Sandwiches (page 171), Herby Date Bites (page 235), and Pizza with Balsamic Tomatoes, Soft Cheese, and Corn Nuts (page 165). You can also thin the cheese a bit with water to create a dip or toss it with pasta and a bit of cooking water as an easy pasta sauce.

2 cups (500 mL) raw cashews, presoaked in just-boiled water for 4 hours

2 tablespoons (30 mL) freshly squeezed lemon juice

1 tablespoon (15 mL) nutritional yeast

1½ teaspoons (7 mL) salt

½ teaspoon (2 mL) garlic powder

2 tablespoons (30 mL) water

½ cup (125 mL) packed fresh flat-leaf parsley, finely chopped

¼ cup (60 mL) packed fresh dill, finely chopped

2 tablespoons (30 mL) finely chopped mint leaves

1 tablespoon (15 mL) minced fresh thyme leaves

Freshly cracked black pepper, to taste

1. Line a small strainer with 2 layers of cheesecloth cut large enough to encase the cheese and set over a medium bowl.

2. Drain and rinse the soaked cashews. Add the cashews to a food processor along with the lemon juice, nutritional yeast, salt, and garlic powder. Blend until the mixture looks like a thick hummus, about 2 minutes. Stop and scrape down the sides of the bowl as needed. With the processor running, drizzle in the water and blend for 30 seconds into a thick dip, not perfectly smooth like a cashew cream.

3. Add the parsley, dill, mint, and thyme. Blend for 30 seconds to incorporate but not fully purée the herbs. Taste and adjust the salt and pepper as needed. More lemon juice will create a fresher, less savoury flavour.

4. Scrape the cheese mixture into the lined strainer. Bring the corners of the cheesecloth together, twist, and secure with an elastic. Transfer the bowl with the strainer to the fridge and allow to strain overnight or up to 24 hours, to remove excess moisture and firm up.

5. Transfer the cheese to an airtight container and store in the fridge for up to 1 week.

Miso Caramel Sauce

Makes about 1 cup (250 mL)

Gluten-Free

Nut-Free

Vegan

1 cup (250 mL) pitted Medjool or Deglet Noor dates (see Note)

¾ cup (175 mL) unsweetened oat milk

1 tablespoon (15 mL) pure maple syrup

2 teaspoons (10 mL) white miso (see Note)

2 teaspoons (10 mL) pure vanilla extract

¼ teaspoon (1 mL) salt

Miso makes everything better with salty, umami depth, including this date caramel sauce. This recipe works best in a bullet blender because it's a small volume, but it will also work in a high-speed blender with a little patience and lots of scraping. It's worth it! Use this in the Mini Cashew Cheesecakes with Miso Caramel Swirl (page 270), over vegan ice cream, as a dip for fruit, or spread on toast.

1. If your dates look dry or a bit too firm, soak them in hot water for 10 minutes. Drain and squeeze out excess water before using.

2. Blend the dates in a bullet blender or high-speed blender on low speed to break them up. Add the oat milk, maple syrup, miso, vanilla, and salt. Blend on medium-low speed until smooth, 2 to 3 minutes. Stop and scrape down the sides of the bowl every 30 seconds. If the sauce is too thick, add 1 to 2 tablespoons (15 to 30 mL) more oat milk. The caramel should be thick but pourable. Taste and adjust the salt if needed. Store in an airtight container in the fridge for up to 4 days.

Note: The flavour of dates and miso vary and will affect the flavour of this caramel (it happened to me!). Trust your tastebuds. If you notice any bitterness or it tastes flat, try adding 1 tablespoon (15 mL) of pure maple syrup or an extra pinch of salt.

Miso Pecan Butter

Makes about 1 cup (250 mL)

Gluten-Free

Vegan

2 cups (500 mL) raw pecans

3 tablespoons (45 mL) red miso

1 tablespoon (15 mL) pure maple syrup

3 tablespoons (45 mL) hot water

Rich red miso adds an enormous depth of flavour to fresh pecan butter, which is surprisingly simple to make! One batch of this butter will make both the Brussels Sprouts with Apple and Miso Pecan Butter (page 69) and the Soba with Miso Pecan Butter (page 141). You can also use this butter spread on sandwiches or thin it out to drizzle over roasted vegetables or tofu.

1. Preheat the oven to 300°F (150°C). Line a baking sheet with parchment paper.

2. Scatter the pecans on the prepared baking sheet and toast until fragrant, about 8 to 10 minutes. Remove from the oven and let the pecans cool on the baking sheet for 5 minutes. Toss the pecans into a food processor and blend until a smooth butter forms, 7 to 8 minutes. Stop and scrape down the sides of the bowl once or twice.

3. In a small bowl, whisk together the miso, maple syrup, and hot water. Add a dollop of pecan butter and whisk thoroughly. Add another dollop of pecan butter and whisk again. Add the remaining pecan butter and whisk until smooth and creamy. (If the mixture seizes and becomes too thick to mix, you can drizzle in a bit of avocado oil to fix it.) Use immediately or transfer to an airtight container and store in the fridge for up to 1 week. The texture will change when stored. Revive the sauce by warming it in a small saucepan over medium-low heat until it looks creamy again.

But I Can't Eat That: Helpful Swaps to Make Your Own Magic

Central to my nutrition philosophy is that the least restrictive path to feeling really good is the healthiest way to go. When I was studying to become a dietitian, a vegan diet was often—inaccurately—labelled as restrictive by those unfamiliar with it. Those times, luckily, are long gone: plant-based and vegan diets have been recognized as not just safe but beneficial for all.

The plant world is incredibly abundant, and these days eating a plant-based diet is really about swaps. Anything you can make, I can make from plants. I find that this is a helpful mindset shift should allergies or intolerances keep you away from any of the plant staples found in this book.

As a dietitian who worked with clients with chronic inflammatory and digestive diseases for more than a decade, adjusting a diet to suit individual tolerance is one of my strong suits. You may or may not have noticed how many of the recipes contained in this book are gluten free or low FODMAP. It's not because these are "healthier" ways to eat; it's that after working with folks with celiac disease and irritable bowel syndrome (IBS) for so long, I want plant-based eating to be accessible to everyone.

But what if you have an allergy to nuts? Or soy? Or you just don't like eggplant? I want to offer some solutions here to help you adapt these recipes to suit you.

First things first: if an ingredient won't change the structure or the flavour of the recipe too much, just omit it or swap it out! For many of the salads, soups, and stews, you can just straight up change the seeds, fruits, or vegetables to something you (a) like, (b) tolerate, or (c) have on hand. Swapping a pumpkin seed for a walnut is not going to change your salad all that much.

But sometimes, particularly in sauces and baking, swapping an ingredient can cause a recipe to fail or at least not taste the same. So I've compiled a list of swaps to help you customize the recipes to accommodate your dietary needs and preferences. You might need to tweak things a bit, by adding an extra pinch of sugar here or a dash of nutritional yeast there, but things should work out.

If you find yourself in a low-FODMAP moment, many of the recipes have suggested swaps.

SWAP THIS	WITH THIS
Ground flaxseed	Ground chia seeds
Peanut butter	Tahini
Salted peanuts	Salted corn nuts or chopped tamari almonds
Cashew butter	Sunflower seed butter
Raw cashews (for making creams)	Raw sunflower seeds (soaked for at least 4 hours in water, then drained) or hemp hearts
Almond flour	Walnut flour
Gluten-free flour blend	Whole-grain flour
Garlic, onions, shallots	Garlic-flavoured low-FODMAP oil or green onions (dark green part only)
Extra-firm tofu	Soy-free store-bought tofu made from chickpeas or fava beans
Tempeh	Extra-firm or pressed tofu or black beans

A Few of My Favourite Things

Putting a home-cooked, plant-powered meal on your plate is the foundation of creating a nourishing way of eating for yourself and your family. You don't need exotic or expensive ingredients to eat well. Healthy eating isn't just for folks who can buy fancy things.

I am also a firm believer that if you have the privilege of choosing the brands you support, do what you can to support small companies that go the extra mile in terms of social justice, sustainability, and quality, as your budget allows. Maybe it's only on special occasions, maybe it's every day. These are just a few of my favourites.

Beans + Grains

Flourist
Canadian-grown beans, grains + freshly milled flours
www.flourist.com

Rancho Gordo
US-based responsibly sourced heirloom beans
www.ranchogordo.com

Flours

Anita's Organic
Canadian organic stone-ground + regular flours
www.anitasorganic.com

Arrowhead Mills

American organic flours, grains, nuts + seeds

www.arrowheadmills.com

Bob's Red Mill

Gluten-free + whole-grain flours + ancient grains

www.bobsredmill.com

Herbs, Teas + Other Magic

Harmonic Arts

Canadian herbs, teas + elixirs

www.harmonicarts.ca

Mountain Rose Herbs

US-based herbs + teas

www.mountainroseherbs.com

Tea Sparrow

Responsibly sourced teas

www.teasparrow.ca

Wooden Spoon Herbs

US-based plant medicines

www.woodenspoonherbs.com

Xálish Medicines

Indigenous-owned plant medicines

www.xalishmedicines.com

Nuts + Seeds

Nut Hut

High-quality, responsibly sourced nuts, seeds + dried fruits

www.nuthut.ca

Prana

Organic, responsibly sourced nuts, seeds + trail mixes

www.pranaorganic.ca

Pasta

Banza
My favourite chickpea-based pasta
www.eatbanza.com

Rummo
Excellent wheat + gluten-free pastas
www.pastarummo.it/en/

Seasonings, Condiments + Oils

Acid League
Canadian-made condiments with a culinary focus
www.acidleague.com

Amano Foods
Canadian-made miso + tamari
www.amanofoods.ca

Diaspora Co
Responsibly sourced high-quality spices
www.diasporaco.com

Maldon Salt
My favourite flaky sea salt
www.maldonsalt.co.uk

Sweets

Camino
Worker-owned, responsibly sourced cocoa
www.camino.ca

Wholesome
Responsibly sourced sweeteners
www.wholesomesweet.com

Acknowledgments

You know what feels like magic? The fact that you are holding this
book in your hands right now. I am beyond grateful to each and
every one of you reading this. It is because you bought this book,
or borrowed it from the library, that I have been able to do work
that I love while still providing for my family.

When I was eighteen, I dreamt of writing a bestselling nutrition
book, and sometimes I can hardly believe that I actually did it! I
know, I know, I should probably have more faith in myself, but
honestly, if you had told me in 2017 that I would spend the next
five years writing three cookbooks, I would not have believed you.
For those of you who have been with me since my one-hit-wonder
of a cooking show, *The Urban Vegetarian*, it is not an overstatement to say that I am here because of you. You have watched my
cooking skills (but not my knife skills, ha!) grow over time, and
despite my firmly self-deprecating tendencies, I might have to
admit that I know how to cook.

But none of this happens in a vacuum. Jim, my love, thank you for trusting and supporting me when I was working until midnight and making all these investments in a business that is essentially a few lines of code on the internet and inches of shelf space. To Elliott and Iris, I hope you see that if this is possible for me, then anything is possible for you. I love you so much sometimes I think my heart will explode. Thank you for eating all of the things that were not your favourite. To my mom, Ligia, there are no words for all the ways you support me and my family. The babysitting, the Donald's runs because I forgot one more dang ingredient, and knowing that somehow this kid of yours would actually make something of herself someday. Svein and Wendy, thank you for always making me feel like a real live Nielsen. I won the in-laws lottery with you and am grateful for all the ways you love and care for us.

A big thank you to all of my friends for their tireless moral support, understanding when my deadlines got in the way, allowing themselves to get roped in over the years as recipe testers and even cookbook models, plus all the ad nauseum strategy sessions about how to make a living by farting around on the internet: Michelle and Jason Kurtz, Payam and Pardeep Fouladianpour, Kelly Boulay, Yvonne Conners and Chris Zaritsky, Michelle Reid and Jon Cartwright, Lindsay Pleskot, Jess Pirnak, Katherine Herringer, Abby Langer, Tori Wesszer, Zach Berman, Jamila Kanji, Sophia McKenzie, Andraya Avison. Now that this one's done, it's time to get a social life.

The reason why this book looks like it does is thanks to two of the most talented people I know: Sophia MacKenzie, who took care of prop + food styling, and Gabriel Cabrera, who worked his magic with a camera. I love you guys super mega—being lucky enough to work with you means that the universe most definitely has my back. Andraya Avison and Camille Lyu, thank you for helping me cook and clean on shoot days because you made this chaos way more enjoyable. To the amazing team at Penguin Random House Canada, thank you for your tireless support and for making such dang cute books.

Finally, to the two women who make my book life possible: Carly Watters, my powerhouse lit agent, and Andrea Magyar, my incredible editor at Penguin Canada. Carly, you inspire me with your intelligence, ambition, and excellent taste in shoes. It is an honour. Andrea, thank you for championing my work, for never flinching when I get "an idea" about what that work is going to look like, or when I ask for another extension! I am eternally in awe of all that you do.

Index